From My Saddle Life Is A Great Adventure

Rod Welling

Published by LPMI, 2023.

Dedication

To

"Magnificent Montana,"

"Glamorous Jesse"

And

"The Great Bobbinski."

Without you I would have never truly experienced the pleasure of trail riding.

Notes from the Author

———

I do not profess to be a professional writer, horseman, clinician, trainer, veterinarian, farrier, comedian, or any other profession I may mention or that the reader may perceive I mention, in this memoir. All opinions and comments are solely from my perspective and strictly for entertainment purposes only. Nothing should be taken as professional advice.

I started my journey into horsemanship at the spry age of sixty-two, the age when most sensible horsemen would be looking hard at retiring. This memoir is my amateur attempt to humorously share some of my memories and adventures during my first nine-years of learning how to ride a horse.

It is my desire to strive to be the best horseman I can for every horse I come in contact with. I know there will come a day when I will no longer be able to swing my leg over the saddle, but hopefully not for a while yet. When the Good Lord does finally call me home, I am sure I will find other horsemen to swap tall tales and humous stories with and most likely still learn something new about horses......

The Memories

Shaken not Stirred.

On Top of Ole Smoky

The Gentleman Ca'boy

As the Crow Hops

The Great Bobbinski

How Far to the Gate

Over the Meadow.

Tail of the Crupper

He's Gonna Hit the Wall

Practical Use

Hang On Beanie Boy

Epiphany

Enter the GPS App

The "F" Trail

That's a Go for Throttles Up

Just Something about a Horse

José

———

IT IS A MOTIVATIONAL TWENTY-NINE DEGREE Saturday morning in early January. The forecast says it will eventually work its way up to a balmy thirty-eight degrees. For this time of year in northwestern Pennsylvania that is extremely moderate, considering there would normally be well over a foot of snow on the ground with temperatures somewhere below freezing. Hearing the forecast, we decided last evening to load up our horses on the day trailer and haul them out for a ride by eleven o'clock this morning.

I may sometimes think I'm able to run with the big dogs, but it is mornings like this that my body reminds me I'm not quite as young as I once was.

My day is starting out with a couple of Tylenol and lots of water, compliments of the time I spent working with Bobbi in the arena yesterday. It took me quite a while, but I am finally beginning to understand there is a symbiotic relationship between the arena and the trail. I am beginning to understand more clearly the advantage of being able to work productively in the arena to improve my abilities, then seeing the rewards of that work being put to practical use on the trail. In the arena, I can choose what I need to focus on and set the time aside to practice until I am proficient at a particular task while in a controlled environment. On the trail however, I am rarely afforded the luxury of time and I am definitely not offered a controlled environment-the trail chooses what to throw my way at any given time.

As the morning wanes and the pain reliever finally starts to kick in, the discomfort in my body is starting to be overshadowed by the anticipation of today's ride.

My wife and I live for riding trails, and this will be our third haul out trail ride of the new year. So far, today is shaping up to be an absolutely beautiful, snowy, picturesque day to ride in the forest.

But I'm getting a little ahead of myself.

My memoir actually starts just over nine years ago, in a little restaurant on the border of New York and Pennsylvania.

MY WIFE DEIRDRE AND I were relaxing at the bar enjoying our after-dinner cocktails. She was excitedly rambling on about a recent trail riding adventure she had been invited to go on with a friend. Her enthusiasm about her adventure was becoming a little contagious as it jogged some old memories of my minor brush with horses when I was in my early teens. I sat listening intently as she excitedly shared her tales.

I have always known my wife loved horses. Over the twenty-five wonderful, marvelous, glorious, exceptional years we had been together, she talked about them enough that even a half alert husband with a brain like mine could not help but pick up on that fact. But in the last few weeks since she had been invited to ride, the conversation about horses had picked up noticeably. Noticeably might be a bit dismissive. More like *all the time* would be more accurate.

Ironically, it was also around the same time that our best friend rekindled her childhood adventures in horsemanship by acquiring a new horse of her own. Looking back at it now, I see how Deirdre's love of horses may have been just a little more stimulated at that time.

It was on that fateful October evening, as I sat there engulfed in her excitement listening to her tales, that I ordered our third chilled shot of tequila. It is a tradition for us to celebrate *anything* we do that is above the "norm" for excitement.

FROM MY SADDLE LIFE IS A GREAT ADVENTURE

I toasted her once again on her awesome horseback riding adventure and without any training wheels we bottomed up the shots.

Over the years when she would hint at the possibility of owning horses my response was pretty standard and always, "Ahhh, no."

However, that evening as I sat my empty shot glass down on the bar, my brain was muttering- "Be a polite and loving husband, Rod. It would be such a nice thing to say to her right now."

As the tequila was warming my soul and I reveled in the energy flowing between us, I asked the question that would change the direction my approaching retirement would take in the foreseeable future.

"Do you really want to own horses before you die?" My, oh my. Just add alcohol. José had no sooner helped those words flow effortlessly out of my mouth, when I knew what her answer was going be.

"Yes."

There was a deep silence between us for the next several moments. No one in this world knows me better than my wife. That being said, allowing that silence was a very well calculated move on her part. The seed was planted, and the silence was watering it. She just had to sit there patiently waiting for it to start to sprout.

During that hiatus in our conversation my mind started running through some scenarios. I thought about our life together and how we approach living. We both strongly believe we do not want to ever look back and wish we had done something when we could have, then regret not doing it. Deep down inside I liked horses. Then I thought this could be a fun adventure. We had to board them so how much work could they be?

Then my good ole pal José helped me out again.

"Okay then. I suppose if this is your dream then we best get to it. I would much rather be falling off a horse in my sixties than my seventies." Looking back, maybe I should have left that falling off part out of it.

So, at sixty-two years old I was about to become a horseman along with my wife who was just a mere nine years younger than me.

THINGS MOVED ALONG PRETTY QUICKLY after that evening. Within two weeks, Deirdre had found a place to board two horses that was only fifteen minutes from our house. She made an appointment, and we were off to see the place. Other than because the owners seemed nice and the facility looked well kept, we had no clue why we liked it, so we decided to rent the stalls. Suddenly we had a place to put two horses that we did not own...yet.

When the owner asked us what we had for horses and when we wanted to move in, Deirdre calmly told her, "We don't own them yet, but we will shortly."

Deirdre explained she wanted to make sure we had a place for them before we bought them. Did you know there is a look people have when they realize they are listening to someone who has no clue what they are talking about?

The owner offered to "hold" the stalls for us until we found the horses. My wife would have none of that. She thanked her for the kind offer but insisted we pay to hold them. She assured her she would find two horses to put in those stalls fairly soon. And there was that look again.

I really was not involved in the whole horse buying process. I looked at what Deirdre told me to look at. I went where she told me to go. I read what she told me to read. The only question I had for her was, how were we going to get them from wherever she found them back to the stable?

Once again, I beheld the miracle of a motivated wife. In less than two days she had located a used horse trailer. A short hour or so trip to the dealer and we were the owners of a new/old horse trailer. We had leased two stalls, owned a horse trailer, and still did not own a horse.

The horse dilemma would be solved soon enough.

Trippin

Almost five weeks to the day after José told me I should help fulfill my wife's lifelong dream, we were off to look at and possibly buy two horses. Looking back on that day nine years ago, we didn't know squat about what we were doing. My only involvement was to tell her I wanted a grey horse like Clint Eastwood rode in one of his movies.

Persuading our best friends to travel with us, we set out one wintry day in late November to go see some horses. With our new/old horse trailer in tow, we were off on an eight-hour cruise. The only person in the vehicle that had any practical knowledge of horses that day was our best friend, the one who had just rekindled her horse involvement. My wife had intellectual knowledge from all the reading she had been doing but as far as the two of us guys along for the ride... nada, zip, zero.

I know Deirdre put a lot of serious thought into her process to find horses, specifically that these horses be suited for beginner/novice riders. As we pulled out that morning, I was so looking forward to my grey horse. You can't ride color, cowboy.

We arrived at our first destination to look at a grade, eleven-year-old chocolate brown appaloosa mare named Montana. The family was evolving out of horseback riding as their children grew older, and Montana was the last horse left out of four. Her owner was a seventeen-year-old boy who had reached the point where the dream of four wheels surpassed that of four hooves.

In no time they had her all tacked up and ready to ride.

Ride? Maybe Deirdre had thought about that part before we left, but I surely had not.

Montana's young rider brought her out, mounted up and rode her around the large lawn. We all listened intently as he explained the cues he was using and her responses to them. I did not have a clue what he was telling us, but it sure looked good. Fifteen minutes later he dismounted and offered her to us for a trial ride.

All five foot four inches of my wife was ready to go. The young lad helped her up in the saddle and away they went. From my perspective Deirdre looked pretty good sitting up there on that horse. But then again, she looked good several years back when we were riding my sisters' horses down in Florida, so what do I know, right? Deirdre enjoyed several trips around the yard and dismounted all smiles and giddy.

That made it my turn.

Back in 2014 I enjoyed my beer and chicken wings a touch more than I enjoyed exercise and fitness. At sixty-two I was six-foot and two-hundred-sixty-five pounds of a lot more of something other than muscle. There I was in the middle of a farmhouse lawn staring down a 14.3 hand appaloosa with a saddle.

The first thought on my mind was: "How the hell do I get up there?"

For some odd reason I remembered using the sidestep on my sister's trailer a few years back when we rode her horses. I looked over at our new/old trailer but did not see what I was looking for there. Poop. A quick look around for something to stand on told me that either I John Wayne it up there into the saddle or I don't get up at all. As appealing as the not getting up option was, it was only fleeting. The young seventeen-year-old offered me a "leg up."

A leg up? At seventeen (even at sixty-two) if someone had offered me a "leg up" I can tell you for a fact a horse would never have entered my mind. Maybe it was the look on my face or the fact that I simply did not respond at all and just stood there staring intently at the horse. Either way, he walked over to me and softly said, "Come on, I'll help you up."

The incredible abilities of youth. I have learned over the years it is not just their lack of fear or their ability to bounce without breaking, but the strength of their body. All of which had already evaded me for quite some time at that point in my life. Interlocking his fingers, he offered me a lower stirrup and seemed to effortlessly lift my fat ass up onto that horse. Not even the slightest grunt or moan. I hated him.

Once I was on the horse and firmly established in the saddle, Montana and I went for a little walk. Actually, Montana took *me* for a little walk and to her credit she was rather nice about it. She obviously knew I had no clue what I was doing, but she stayed calm. Me? My heart was racing, my legs were squeezing, and my fingers were white holding the reins. We successfully walked around the lawn for several minutes before she took me toward the only tree within reasonable distance.

She calmly rode me into the branches while I tried to steer her away with the reins. I could hear the chuckles of the young man's father as he commented to my wife, "She's testing him." Then laughter from the entire group. When we eventually came out of the tree, on Montana's terms I might add, not mine, she took me over to the group where I lowered myself off of her back to solid ground.

With my heart still pounding like a hammer in my chest, the young rider and I negotiated the final transaction. In short order I was the proud owner of our first horse, and it was not grey.

Then one of the coolest things I have ever experienced happened. Once Montana was on board, one at a time each of the three family members went into the trailer and took a couple minutes to say goodbye to her. Watching that has stuck with me. Once I started to get to know Montana, I understood why.

With one down and one to go we made a quick stop at Mickey D's to fuel our hunger. After enjoying some delectable culinary delights, we were on our way to the next farm.

While Montana had come from a small family farm with very few amenities, the next place was a large ranch. Pulling up the long entrance we saw huge trailers, equipment, barns, and outbuildings everywhere.

Doc'z was a six-year-old registered bay Quarter Horse mare being sold by a young girl. It was immediately apparent, however, that dad was really in charge of the proceedings. When Deirdre had spoken to the young girl about the horse, she swore the mare was "bomb proof." We have since learned a little bit about that claim.

Dad was the first to meet us as we pulled in. He immediately started telling us all about the horse. Its lineage, its capabilities, its possibilities and why his daughter was selling her. Then he shared some stories about the farm and some of his past horse delivery experiences. Fifteen minutes give or take after we arrived, his daughter finally joined us and we all chatted for a bit longer.

About twenty minutes after we arrived, we were finally led into a huge barn to see the horse. Dad apologized for the delay explaining they had to take a quad out to one of the furthest pastures once we arrived to get her.

She was still out in the furthest pasture, after we called and told them we would be there in an hour? Hmmm. I didn't recall hearing a quad at all. Should have been the first flag.

As we entered the barn, we found the horse all tacked and tied to the wall, calm and relaxed. She was, in fact, a very stunning bay. The young girl then took us through the motions as dad stepped aside. She demonstrated how calm and collected she was. What a mild manner she had. She pulled on her tail, walked under her belly, climbed on and over her, lifted her feet and rode her slowly and calmly around for us.

When I asked about the really soft green poop she dropped while we were standing there, dad was quick to tell us it was the alfalfa she got into that morning in the pasture. In the far away back pasture that you had to take a quad to get her from? Should have been the second flag.

When Deirdre mounted up and rode the horse there was nothing. As inexperienced as my wife was and as young as that horse was there should have been something. She tried to get the horse moving but she was lethargic and just didn't seem to want to go. As an unknowledgeable beginner horseman who had no idea about riding and was looking for a safe "bomb proof" horse, that was not necessarily a bad thing. However, that should have been flag number three.

After some more discussion, and the fact that she was a bay, and Deirdre loves bays, we decided we would take her. Dad and daughter eagerly offered to load her on the trailer for us. We were told earlier that the horse loaded easily, but she didn't load without a little work that morning. At first all the horse did was step on and step off. Then they got a long whip to get her to step up. Then they locked arms across her rump to stop the retreat. When they finally got her in the trailer they couldn't slam and latch the doors fast enough.

That should have been flag number four and we should have terminated the deal and walked away. We did not. Mainly because we were unknowledgeable. Looking back, there were several warning signs that this was not the right horse for us, but we were too inexperienced to see them. All we could think about was the fact there were two horses in our new/old trailer coming home with use to start a new adventure in our lives.

It was late November and winter was just starting to unfold. in northwestern PA. That meant the trail riding season was over, and for the next several months all we could do was visit the horses at the barn and get to know them. The facility we had chosen was just a small farm with six stalls. It had a small 100 x 30-foot run-in attached to the back of the barn where we could work the horses out of the weather.

That is how we started. Every night that winter, and I do mean every night, we went to the barn and walked the horses for a couple of hours. We had no clue what we were doing or what we needed to do, but we loved freezing to death walking those horses in that run-in. We led them around stopping and turning, walking straight lines and figure eights. We would get all giddy and excited when we didn't have to pull on them to make them go, stop, or turn. It was just us, Deirdre & me, our golden retriever Bubba, Montana and Doc'z and the world of horses.

The Run-In

A S THE WEEKS and months rolled on, we started to acquire some tack. Once again, we had no clue what we were doing so our first saddles were less than desirable. We found this smoking deal, two saddles for less than a hundred bucks apiece. Who knew anything about fit, they were saddles. Full quarter horse bars? What's that?

Even being totally ignorant, when we threw those saddles up on the horses the first time, we could clearly see they didn't fit. We learned fairly quickly to start asking more intelligent questions regarding tack. Traveling to a reputable tack shop near us, we invested a little more time and money and got ourselves some more appropriate saddles and bridles.

Our best friend was invaluable. She was constantly helping us learn about everything. Deirdre and I literally read about horses every day and tried to learn as much as we could. We watched endless internet videos and asked countless questions of our friend. That poor girl had to feel inundated, but she still hangs with us, and we are as close as ever.

Then we met the farrier. I don't believe I had even heard that word before. Who would have thought taking care of the feet was that important? Kind of like cars, no wheels, no ride. Our relationship started when we watched him shoe Montana for the first time in her life. It took him over an hour to shoe just the first foot. Just over two and a half hours later she was shod. She has since figured out shoes make her feet feel much better, and now she loves getting her summer PF-Flyers® on. (0)

FROM MY SADDLE LIFE IS A GREAT ADVENTURE

I could seriously write a novel about my farrier. He is well known in our area for being one of the best in his trade. In the nine years I have spent with the man I have learned more about horses than you could possibly imagine. I have spent every visit with him as he cares for our horses. He was an endurance rider for years as well as a farrier. The knowledge, the horsemanship, and the stories he has shared are nothing short of incredible.

He told me recently that of all the people he services, it was people like us he respected the most. Not because I was always there to help and listen but because we ride our horses and enjoy what we are doing. He is in his late seventies and finally looking to retire. His son and grandson are doing more and more and that's okay, he has more than earned his time to relax. I will be eternally grateful for all he has taught me through the years.

Then came learning about hay, feed, supplements, medications, mucking stalls and cleaning up horse poop. What? In my wildest dreams I didn't have a flipping clue this was all part of it, too.

The veterinarian. Well okay then. Who knew they all didn't do business in a little brick building? Who knew you could not make an appointment for just any one of them to come to the barn to see your horse? Who knew you needed to have a vet for a horse, period? Or that some of them actually enjoy eating your horse treats?

By the end of January, I was quickly realizing that house training a puppy was a whole lot easier than owning horses. I "smiled" every time I got in the car and we "headed to the barn."

The days rolled by and traveling back and forth to the barn began to seem endless. The learning seemed dauntless and every day it felt like we learned yet one more important lesson.

I honestly have to say it was not what I thought owning a horse was remotely going to be like. I thought back to my sister in Florida. She had the horses, so I never knew about the boarding. She had the tack, so I never knew about all those parts and pieces. She had the trailer, so I never knew about teaching them to load. She had well-mannered trained horses, so I never knew about the hard work and hours it took to get them there.

No indeed. This was not at all what I thought owning horses would be like.

My vision was more like: "Let's go ride!" "Okay!" And we would get on a horse and go ride.

Whoa Mama. And it's only been six weeks there Ca'boy. I cursed José regularly.

It has now been twelve weeks since we picked up the horses and brought them home. We have the tack pretty well squared away and have some properly fitting gear. We have spent hours tacking and untacking the horses to be sure we are doing everything correctly. We even mounted them a few times in the run-in.

We were ready.

It was a cool February morning, and the sun was shining. Today was the day. We were going to take our first ride around the farm. I mean our first ride, ride. No friends. No help. Just Deirdre and Doc'z, me and Montana. Outside. No walls. No fence. We tacked up the girls in the run-in and excitedly led them outside to the five-gallon bucket turned upside down we were using for a mounting block.

Deirdre moseyed on up to our mounting block and swung right up into the saddle. Wow, look at my woman! So smooth and confident, wearing the biggest smile on her face. Well, I can't let her down now, can I? I had best get up there so we can ride, baby, ride.

I brought Montana to a stop close to the bucket. Awesome. Montana just stood there stone still looking straight ahead, almost like she knew what was going to happen. I arranged the bucket just a bit and then stepped up on it. I lightly put my left foot in the stirrup and put my hands on the horn and the cantle, just like in the video. I saw Montana square up. Wow, really, just like the video!

One, two, three and up I went. I leaned forward a touch. I swung my right leg out and over her hips and started to go and go and GO. The saddle passed six inches under my crotch. My adrenaline must have been a touch higher than I thought.

I suddenly realized that the laws of physics were about to take over. Based on the amount of momentum I had created from my left leg pushing and two my arms pulling, I knew I was not going to stop above the saddle. With a sunken feeling I accepted that gravity was about to take hold of my overweight body. In that nano second, I knew this mounting effort was not going to end well for me.

A moment later I was lying on the ground, on my back, desperately gasping for air. I recollect faintly hearing Deirdre say something. I have no idea what she said because I thought I was going to die lying there on that cold ground. Through the pain and the fear of dying, I somehow remembered the horse. Deep inside of me the thought of a runaway horse popped into my head, and I did not have hold of the reins.

Still gasping I struggled to sit up and grab for the reins, which I didn't see until I looked up at Montana's neck. Oh boy.

What I saw next was burnt into my memory for life. Montana stood there perfectly still, not moving a muscle. She had turned her face and was looking down at me there on the ground. They say horses do not have human responses; I will debate that at times. I swear that horse only had one thought on her mind as she stood there looking down at me.

"What the hell was that?"

I watched helplessly as she ever so slowly just walked away, swaying slightly, her head lowered and what appeared to be shaking back and forth. If she were human, I would have put money on her thoughts being nothing short of: "Oh my Lord, what have I signed on for?"

Suddenly Deirdre replaced Montana in my view as she tried to help me up. I finally heard her asking me if I was alright. Once I started breathing a little easier, I did a quick check list. Other than some sore muscles and a lot of hurt pride I assured her I was fine.

We then spent the next thirty minutes trying to catch Montana. It was our first lesson in Montana's ability to stay just out of reach until she wants to get caught. Once we finally caught her, we figured we'd had enough excitement for one day and decided we should chalk it up as a great learning experience. Maybe work a little more on mastering mounting in the run-in first.

Jesser Roo

O VER THE NEXT COUPLE OF WEEKS, we religiously practiced mounting and riding around in the run-in with no major incidents. Montana was sound and good natured, but we were struggling with Doc'z.

We conferred with some friends and finally decided to hire a young rider/trainer to come work with Doc'z and give us an evaluation. We had done enough research to know that a six-year-old could still be a bit of a handful. We were still under the assumption she was sold to us as relatively 'bomb proof" and safe for a beginner. As the days passed, things were just getting worse and worse. Compared to the day we picked her up she was decidedly not the same horse. Either way it was apparent that something was awry.

It took the trainer less than a week to tell us that Doc'z was "green broke" at best. With our novice riding skills, she obviously would not be a good horse for us. We called the seller back regarding the discovery and we got about as far as the alfalfa poop Doc'z dropped the day we bought her.

Thankfully our best friend, who had been helping us through all of this, had seen a nine-year-old mare for sale by a reputable local dealer. She had taken the liberty to call him and to do some preliminary groundwork about a possible trade. After some conversations between the dealer, our friend and Deirdre, we loaded up Doc'z on the new/old trailer and headed out to do some horse trading.

With a little negotiation a deal was struck, and with a little more cash outlay we now owned a nine-year-old registered palomino quarter horse we named Jesse.

Life was much better on the ranch after that. Jesse was much more personable and well trained than Doc'z. Sporting our new saddles and tack we finally got a chance to start wandering out of the run-in and around the lawns and fields surrounding the farm. We were both devoid of any riding skills, so we weren't very adventurous on our rides. We kept very close to the barn as we tried out the horses in the great outdoors. We may have really sucked as riders, but we sure had that yank to turn, pull to stop and kick to go almost figured out.

We were now "officially" horse owners and solidly classified as "novice riders." Wahoo! It was time to get some more insight on the area around the farm where we could possibly ride. Our waitress friend, who started this whole adventure by letting Deirdre ride one of her horses, was kind enough to set up a ride out of our barn with a young lady who lived just down the road from where we were boarding. On the day of the ride, we met a new friend, who would ultimately become a very good friend over the years. We explained to her we were new riders and she assured us she did "new" good. She then proceeded to do just that.

Using our newly purchased two step mounting block, we mounted up and were ready to go. We were so excited. Our little group of four riders headed out the lower part of one of our farm's pastures and into the woods onto some trails. We meandered about through the woods for a bit before coming out in the far corner of another pasture where we swooped around that corner and went right back into the woods. We continued to ride on more easy-to-follow trails, exiting the woods once again as we skirted the edge of another pasture, until we reached a secondary traffic road.

Along our journey our trail boss kept us informed as to where we were while she also explained some basic riding etiquette regarding riding through pastures or lawns. She imparted a lot of information to us that day. Although our ears let it all in, our minds were so focused on the ride we only retained a part of it all.

We rode the secondary road for quite some time before we finally re-entered back into the woods. At that point I sort of knew where I might be in relationship to our barn, but in all honesty, if I had to point to where it was, I probably would not have been correct. But what I do remember and will never forget is leaving the trail and starting to descend into a shallow runoff ravine.

It was late winter, and spring was knocking loudly on the door. Most of the snow was gone except for a few left-over patches scattered about here and there that were shaded from the sun. The wide trails we were on earlier had been conducive to easy riding, but now the trail just seemed to disappear. We were starting a descent into a rocky runoff with wet, loose rocks and occasional snow patches. Hmmm.

I had a moment of panic as I looked where we were about to go, then suddenly we were in motion and starting down. I had no clue what kind of horse Montana was as far as her tolerance of ignorant riders. Thinking back on that ride down that runoff, and what she tolerated from me, makes me respect a good horse with a tolerant personality.

I had no idea how to sit a horse properly. I could not even tell you what "give her her head" meant in the horse world. And if someone said to me "don't brace," I would have thought, "against what? there's nothing here." I won't even mention breathing because, well I just won't. All I knew was that if I made it to the bottom of that runoff and I was still alive, I may have to reconsider this whole horseback riding thing.

Like a true "newbie" I did what I needed to do to survive. I wrapped my legs so tight around that horse I was amazed she could even breathe. My body was so tight, trying not to fall off (braced) that every muscle in my body was screaming at me. I pulled the reins back to my chest (not giving her her head) and just kept yelling "Whoa."

Somewhere along the descent our trail boss finally had enough of me telling my horse to whoa and yelled back to me, "Whoa is the stop command. Say EASY." Who would have thunk?

Hearing my wife's loud voice of panic, I forced myself to look up from directly under my horse as I caught the last of her fall off Jesse. Everyone immediately stopped and to my thrill Montana just followed the crowd without me having to reach my hands over my head and pull her jaw out of its socket. Our trail boss had already dismounted, making sure Deirdre was okay. Ascertaining that there was no physical harm to human or horse, it was time to get back up and continue.

Remember that new mounting block? Yep, so now what? Thank goodness the trail boss was on top of what Deirdre was thinking because she quickly offed her a leg up. In short order we were moving again and, on our way, back to the barn. Other than a few frayed nerves we survived the runoff, thank God.

It would be some time before we would challenge that runoff again, but we now had some other trails we could ride. That ride eventually inspired us to have enough courage to explore some of the other trails we had seen in the woods close to our barn. It would certainly be the catalyst to our life of trail riding.

I Got This

O VER THE NEXT COUPLE OF MONTHS, we began to
wander out more often on our own into the woods around the
barn. With each ride we became more and more confident until one
evening whilst at the restaurant enjoying our after-dinner cocktails, we
decided we would trailer the horses out and meet our waitress friend
for a ride. The plan was simple; I would load the horses and haul them
to the trailhead and Deirdre would bring a change of clothes and meet
us there after work. I think José was out target shooting with my Silver
Bullets that night and one must have hit me. Not sure what I was
thinking when I agreed to that plan but it sure as hell wasn't based on
my knowledge of loading horses.

Maybe it was precipitated by the fact we had just traded our new/old
horse trailer for a brand new one. I had discovered that, apparently,
the quick fix in the trailer industry sometimes involves cosmetically
repairing trailers and then letting the next guy figure it out. Just one of
the many lessons I have learned along this journey.

When the day arrived, I got the trailer hooked up to the truck and
headed to the barn. I rounded up the horses from the pasture, tied
Montana to the side of the trailer then proceeded to load Jesse first.

I had never, ever loaded a horse onto a trailer by myself before that
day, but I stayed at a Holiday Inn Express once. (1) With Jesse in tow, I
casually walked up behind the trailer and stepped up into the left side
stall. Taking a couple steps in, I turned and gave the lead line a little
pull and Jesse started to follow me in. As she stepped up and put her
two front feet into the trailer, I backed up keeping some pressure on
the lead as I got out of her way. She took a step or two more, then with

about half of her body inside the trailer she decided to suddenly reverse direction and back out.

Wrong direction. You need to come forward. I yanked and pulled hard on the lead to make her move forward. Then she brought her head up to resist. Oh no you don't. I need you to come forward. So, I yanked and pulled harder. Her head instantly went up as she went up. Her head hit the top of the trailer then she lurched back out. I had the entire weight of my body pulling on the lead rope when she suddenly dropped onto her haunches and tumbled over backwards yanking the lead rope out of my hands and leaving me with two of the nicest rope burns you could imagine. I watched in horror as she flipped over backward then rolled onto her side and stopped moving.

Holy Shit! I just killed my wife's horse.

My heart stopped as I stood there stunned. Jesse just laid there for what seemed like an eternity, then she moved, got organized and stood up. Suddenly I realized I needed to get the lead rope, so I quickly scrambled off the trailer and picked up the lead.

I did a quick check of the horse and did not see any injuries, so I walked her around a bit to be sure. As we walked, I took that opportunity to allow both our heart rates to come back to a more normal level.

Once I felt semi composed, I got back to the task at hand which was to load the horses. I walked back over toward the trailer with Jesse in hand and before I could even step up, she planted her feet. I mean she planted those feet.

Tug-of-War between an eleven-hundred-pound horse and a two hundred- and sixty-five-pound man. Odds are about eighty to one the man will win. After a couple of failed attempts to load Jesse, I decided that maybe I should get Montana on first and then Jesse might go on more easily. Seemed like a logical choice, right?

I tied Jesse on the opposite side of the trailer and got Montana. Montana thought she might increase those odds a bit to be sure. As I walked up to the trailer with her in tow, she didn't just stop, she pulled me twenty feet back. Not once, not twice but three times before I realized I just might be in over my head here. Yep, odds were definitely in the horses favor to win. Thanks for confirming that, Montana.

At that point I was just overly grateful that I did not have to tell my wife I killed her horse, so I tucked my tail between my legs and put the girls back out in the pasture. With a shattered ego and battered pride, I wandered off into the field searching for that one exact spot that gave me a single bar of service on my cellphone. I texted everyone to let them know hauling out was not going to happen that day. With profound sadness I got in my truck and headed home and lived to fight another day.

"Loading is not a horse problem it is a leading problem."

It would be in the distant future before I would hear that phrase for the first time. It would also be one of many phrases I would learn in the years to come. But on that day, it was not in my data base. It would take us a little more than a year before we started to learn how to get the horses to trailer load. It would take another year to understand it and then another couple to be able to do it proficiently.

Tree Weaving

THE NEXT SEVERAL MONTHS slowly moved on. Deirdre and I spent a lot of time riding in the woods adjoining the barn, never straying too far. Our primary focus was staying on the horses as they moved because we certainly spent our share of time falling off. Trying to figure out a way to re-mount after we fell off, instead of walking all the way back to the barn to the mounting block, was also high on our to-do list. They say that a horse has the closest gait to humans of any other animal. At that point in time, I wasn't seeing it.

Deirdre seemed to spend a little more time coming off then I did. Jesse is a quick horse, but keep in mind, at that point quick to us to was anything faster than a snail's pace. Combine that with not knowing anything about proper equitation definitely did not help keep us in the saddle during sudden spooks, turns, slips, or trips.

One of our favorite things to do at that time was "Tree Weaving." We would ride out then go off the trail into the woods and wander around. We would weave around trees, step over dead fall, duck under branches, follow each other around and try to maneuver the horses through minor obstacles. An experienced rider would have probably been bored to tears, but it was more or less giving us objectives indirectly tied to a sense of accomplishment. We had no clue what we were doing but it was helping us to learn how to get around okay.

ONE SUNNY AFTERNOON we were slowly working our way back to the barn after an hour or so on the trails and doing some "Tree Weaving", when something spooked Jesse dumping Deirdre in a pile of soft moss.

Hearing the commotion behind me, I turned to see Deirdre slowly getting up as Jesse stood about fifteen feet away watching her. Give or take a few moments, Jesse decided she was done with the ride and was just going to go home without her rider. She turned and calmly headed off into the woods.

After confirming Deirdre was okay for the fourth or fifth time, while watching Jesse start to fade away into the woods, Deirdre told me, "Go get my horse."

"But?"

"I'm fine. I will walk back to the road and work my way back to the barn. Now, GO GET MY HORSE."

A smart husband knows when a discussion is no longer a discussion. I may not be that bright sometimes, but I was bright enough then. Off into the woods Montana and I went following her horse.

You all remember that I am still a brand-new rider here, right?

Montana and I were soon bushwhacking through the woods, chasing Jesse. I had absolutely no clue what I was going to encounter, or how I was going to handle it when I did encounter it. However, once this adventure concluded, I learned the value of trusting your horse and how valuable that relationship can be. I know horses are incapable of human reactions, but they are capable of something that connects them to their riders.

Within minutes, Montana and I found ourselves in brush so thick I would not have hiked through it with my dog. I was scared to death to pull or kick or even touch Montana because I did not want to come off. I started to hold my breath more and more as I gently tried to lead her left or right with the reins. Fortunately, Montana somehow understood our mission was to catch Jesse and just took it all in stride.

She maneuvered us around and through everything with relative ease, not once putting me in a bad position in the saddle. When we came upon a cluster of broken branches and small tree limbs we had to navigate through, she calmy and slowly just picked her way through it.

When my foot got knocked from the stirrup she would just stop, without being asked, and wait as I regained my footing. At one point I had to lay back in the saddle to get under a branch. As soon as we cleared it, she just stopped, half looked back at me, and waited for me to get back upright in the saddle. Then we were off again. Overall Montana was way calmer than I was.

Jesse continued to steadily put some distance between us, but we never lost sight of her. After thirty minutes of bushwhacking, we finally caught up to her at the bottom of a large ravine. She was standing there contemplating climbing a 250-foot high, 50-degree embankment. Montana and I stood there and watched her make three unsuccessful attempts to climb before she resigned herself to going with us. I dismounted, picked up her reins and tied her to the rear D-ring on Montana's saddle.

Once she was secure, I had to figure out how to get from our current location, wherever that was, back to the barn. I would ultimately realize Jesse had the right direction with the embankment, the barn was less than a half mile away. Obviously that route was out, and I sure wasn't going back the same way we just came. Ultimately, I decided to walk downstream about a quarter of a mile where I knew the trail crossed it. I was scared to death to get back up and ride, which was probably a blessing in disguise as I obviously had no clue how to correctly pony a horse.

As I was working my way downstream leading Montana with Jesse in tow, Montana suddenly yanked her head up pulling the reins from my hand. She then immediately proceeded to step on one and snapped it off at the bit. Well, that sucks! No big deal, I wasn't going to ride anyway, I'll just use the other rein to lead her.

With the intact rein in hand, we proceeded to walk about ten more feet when Montana stopped again. This time she refused to move forward. Now what?

No matter what I tried I could not get her to move her feet. I started to get a bit excited and nervous. Big breath in, big breath out. Inhale, exhale. Stay calm and relax, I said to myself. I took a bottle of water from my saddle bag and tried to calmly figure out what to do. I talked to Montana about what was going on as I took a couple of sips of my water, wishing it was a fine scotch. When I reached up to scratch the side her neck, she took a couple of small steps and gently nudged me to the right, away from the stream. I started to correct her, but I noticed something to the right. Looking more closely I could make out what appeared to be a game trail, only bigger.

It looked tight but useable. The brush was not thick, and it was basically heading in the direction we needed to go. As I stepped toward the trail with lead in hand to check it out more closely, Montana stepped out right behind me. Within about twenty feet, the trail opened up and we were on an old road of some type that was very easy to walk. The road switched back a couple of times, but twenty-minutes later I found myself at the bottom of our pasture. That little maneuver probably cut off about 30 minutes of hiking time from the way I originally wanted to go. Well, I'll be a monkey's uncle.

Here comes the lesson. Unbeknownst to me, I think Montana and I were communicating to each other during that entire event. Then the trail thing she did. Don't get me wrong, if I had not felt comfortable walking that trail, I would not have. The fact remains that she saw the trail and I didn't. How did she know where that trail went? She had never been on that trail before that day, or since. The moment I turned onto that trail, she relaxed and slowly walked behind me or beside me the rest of the way home.

From that day on, I started talking to my horse whenever we faced situations we needed to get through together.

Solo

⸺

AMAZING ANIMALS THESE HORSES. One day they make you feel like you're the king of the world, and the next they knock you down so low you can see the roots of the grass. On one beautiful day when Deirdre had to work, she convinced me to take Montana out by myself for a little ride. Oh, you are a silly, silly man.

I was not really keen on the idea of riding a horse alone in the middle of nowhere. I suppose that might have seemed a bit paranoid to some riders, but I suspect the years I had spent scuba diving imbedded the "never dive alone" mantra into my thick skull and it just seemed to effortlessly roll over into horseback riding and it was going to be an absolutely gorgeous spring day.

"I wish you didn't have to work so we could ride today." From the moment I uttered those words, Deirdre relentlessly encouraged me to go out anyway. She ultimately convinced me that I could handle it, so another page in my horsemanship saga was about to be written.

Somewhere between "I don't know about that" and "That's really not a good idea" lays "Why the hell not."

So later that morning, Montana and I found ourselves in the woods behind the barn. Thanks to all the tree-weaving we had been doing over the previous couple of months, we had become familiar with a large area in which to ride. On the upside, I felt comfortable that I would not be far from the barn. On the downside, I was nervous about riding alone. What I learned soon enough is that just because you are familiar with the terrain does not mean you are familiar with the wildlife.

Montana and I were approaching the predetermined point I had chosen where we would turn and start working our way back toward the barn. Everything so far had been going remarkably well. I actually found myself feeling relaxed enough to take some pictures along the way. Montana and I were slowly navigating our way up a slight grade to a "T" in the trail where we would make a right to start back home, when Mother Nature screamed; "HELLO."

If you have never fallen off a horse, then you do not know that it defies all known physical laws of the universe by actually slowing down time.

Suddenly, a grouse took off out of the scrub on our right. Montana dropped down on her front legs and launched to the left.

I heard the noise from the grouse, and I immediately felt my heart thump deep and hard in my chest.

I felt Montana drop. Bada boom. Bada boom.

I felt Montana move to the left. Bada boom. Bada boom.

I felt my butt go left with Montana. Bada boom. Bada boom.

I realized my torso was not following my butt. Bada boom. Bada boom.

I felt gravity pulling my torso to the ground as my butt departed the saddle. Bada boom. Bada boom.

I felt the impact of my body as it came in contact with good old Mother Earth. Bada boom. Bada boom.

I felt dazed and confused as I laid there on the ground. Bada boom. Bada boom.

Two point five seconds of extreme slow motion and I clearly captured every minute detail.

A quick assessment told me I would most likely be a little sore the next day, but I was not broken, always a good thing. Montana? I realized I needed to find my horse. Looking around, I saw her about fifty feet away eating grass. Whew. I slowly worked myself up off the ground and wandered over and she let me catch her right off. Amazing.

Once I had Montana, I needed to figure out how I was going to get back up on her. We were still not very proficient at remounting while out in the woods. Once we got in the saddle to ride, we tried to stay in the saddle until we got back. Therefore, I did not have a lot of experience at finding something appropriate to stand on. Ground mounting was absolutely out of the question. Even if I could get my fat leg up high enough to put my foot in the stirrup, I didn't have enough strength to pull myself up. I knew I needed to find a large log or rock to give me some height. Looking around, I did not see anything in our immediate vicinity that would fit the bill, so we started to walk the trail back toward the barn. And a barren trail it was for something to stand on to mount.

Eventually I spied a little ditch. If I could coax her down into the ditch, it might give me just enough height. With a little work, I finally got her to walk down into the ditch and stand still as I grabbed my left leg and helped it up into the stirrup. One bounce, two bounce, three bounces and up I went, then suddenly realized that I was no Matt Dillion. It took every ounce of strength I had just to get my left leg straight, and I hadn't even started to swing my right leg up and over her back yet.

I leaned my stomach over the saddle to try to get some momentum to swing my right leg over, when Montana decided she'd had enough of this circus and started to walk off. There I was, looking like a dead body slung over a horse in a movie, being brought in for the reward. But nobody was leading my horse.

I couldn't stay there, and I couldn't get her to stop. So, I tried to get down, and I fell off my horse again. Only this time she never stopped walking, she just kept on going.

I followed her for a spell, maintaining about a twenty-foot distance, while she walked just fast enough that I could not catch her. I think she did it on purpose, that snot. Eventually she picked up the pace, and soon she was out of sight. There I was in yet another new situation. I had no clue how I was going to find her. As I walked the trail back to the barn, I thought about what I was going to say when I called that very short list of people I knew that might help me find my horse.

Forty minutes later, I came up over the grade behind our pasture and found Montana standing next to the fence with Jesse. My heart raced as I realize it was a miracle, a divine miracle! For the second time on that ride, I collected my horse after falling off. This time I decided that I would just walk the rest of the way home.

First Big Ride

A S WE CONTINUED TO RIDE around our farm, friends would occasionally haul in and ride with us, but most of the time it was just Deirdre and me. Deirdre was the internet horse video junky; she would share what she had learned, and we would take that newfound knowledge out into the woods. Sometimes we got it and sometimes we didn't, never really knowing if we were doing things the right way. Either way, win or lose, we were having the time of our lives.

We were learning more about horses all the time from any resource we could find. From the owner of the barn about feed, basic care and mucking stalls to our vet and farrier and all the knowledge they had to impart. From the equine dentist to friends who had owned and ridden horses since childhood. If someone knew about horses, we would talk and listen. Looking back, we started to become sponges soaking up anything we could learn. As we gained more and more knowledge, we eventually understood that there is rarely such a thing as bad advice about horsemanship, just differences in individual viewpoints or beliefs. It would be up to us to decipher all that information and develop our own direction as to how we wanted to use it.

In July of that first summer, we got our first lesson about broken bones from working with horses. Not that it is much of an honor BUT Deirdre proudly holds the distinction of breaking first. We were letting the horses into the run-in when one of them pinned Deirdre to the wall which initiated a fall resulting in a broken arm. This would be the first of several trips to the hospital with breaks that involved the horses.

With Deirdre's arm broken our riding slowed considerably, but she insisted we needed to stay in contact with the horses. I guess so they would not forget who we were or something. We still didn't know what we were doing as far as "groundwork" was concerned, but as she healed, we kept in contact with the horses just about every day. With all that extra time on her hands as she recovered, she researched more. It seemed like she was never out of new ideas for us try. I did what any good, married Ca'boy would do, what he was told, silently.

———

WE FINALLY GOT DEIRDRE MENDED and back up on her horse and were once again back out in the woods behind the barn. In late fall the neighbor, who had taken us on our first ride around the barn, invited us to join a group ride she organized from her place down to the lake and back.

The invitation was extremely exciting, but we were leery about accepting. Real world, our track record for staying on our horses for an entire ride, although getting better, still was not faring very well. The offer stood open should we decide to go, we just had to show up before they left on the day of the ride. We had a week to think it over before deciding.

On the day of the ride, the infamous "why not" approach Deirdre has down to a science won out, and we rode through the woods to meet up with the group just as they were getting ready to head out.

On the way over to join the group, half of me was wishing they had already gone, and the other half was excited to go on our first "long" ride. Once we got there and found they had not departed, the trail boss excitedly welcomed us. In a matter of minutes, the entire group made us feel so welcome and comfortable that my thoughts turned solely to the adventure that awaited us.

True to form, less than a half of a mile into the ride Deirdre fell off Jesse.

Everyone quickly tried to corral Jesse, but she out foxed them all and just trit-trotted her big ole palomino self, right back down the trail toward the barn. The trail boss directed us all to stay where we were and wait for her to return as she set out to retrieve Jesse. We all watched her depart in a canter back down the trail hot on Jesse's heels.

Twenty minutes later she returned, riding Jesse with her horse in tow. Apparently, Jesse had evaded capture all the way back to the barn. As the story goes, once they reached the barn, the trail boss explained to Jesse that the choices she had made were totally unacceptable and that there were going to be no more such shenanigans. I am speculating now, but I believe the quiz for that lecture she gave Jesse had been administered on the way back to the group.

Deirdre remounted her steed, and we were back underway. It wasn't long after that I got my first lesson in horsemanship diplomacy. While we were riding along on an old logging road, we were met by the landowners.

Our trail boss was in front and graciously rode up to meet them. It was obvious just by their body language that the landowners were not pleased to see us. I quietly watched and listened as they firmly explained that we were on private property and were not allowed to ride there. Our trail boss conveyed our deepest apologies while expressing that we would never intentionally ride where we were not welcome. I watched as she effortlessly soothed the situation. It was like listening to a fine-tuned negotiator. When those folks came out to meet us, they were loaded for bear and ready to shoot. When we left, they were pleasant, understanding, and willing to forgive our transgressions. Impressive it was indeed.

Once we were off the property and on a different trail, I commented to our trail boss how impressed I was with her handling of the situation. She proceeded to explain to all of us that, trail riding on any land we do not personally own is a privilege, and we should always respect that privilege. We should never get into an argument with a landowner. Always suck up no matter how bad it may seem.

And I quote: "Sometimes a little kiss ass and suck up may just get you the permission you never sought in the first place." I liked this girl.

As we continued our adventure down another old forest road, we came upon a section that had been washed out. Today, neither Deirdre nor I would think twice about navigating that wash-out. But at that moment, it had "Falling Off the Horse" written all over it in capital letters.

With the help of the trail boss, Deirdre gave it a try but ended up getting down and walking the horse through it. As for me, I just plain did not want to try it. Nor was I keen about getting off my horse, because getting back up was still highly problematic for me.

My attitude created a little bit of a situation. We were far enough into the ride that the group was not going to go back. I had no choice, I had to address that obstacle one way or another. The trail boss asked me, "If you don't want to walk it and don't want to ride it, then how would you get by it?"

I was prepared for the question. I had been waiting near the back of the group looking at my options. Up and around. Another rider and I proceeded to go up the side of the mountain, bushwhack our way around and come down on the far side of the washout. Looking back now at our approach to that difficult situation, riding the obstacle would have been much easier and safer. I commend the patience of the trail boss and the other riders that day, because if I watched me do that now, I would think I was nuts.

Once we arrived at the lake, the group took a break to stretch, and everyone dismounted. Well, not everyone. Unless I had a very high log, getting back up would be nearly impossible. Scanning the surrounding area, I did not see anything I could stand on that would be high enough, so I figured I was better off just staying on my horse.

After the break, we rode single file through a boggy area toward a very steep twenty-foot-high bank we had to climb. It was, for me, far worse than the wash out as a challenge, only this time there were no other options. I watched the trail boss ascend it and felt as if my heart was in my throat. When our turn came, the trail boss yelled down to us. "Lean forward, grab some main, and let the horse go." I threw out those shorts when I got home that night, just sayin.

We traveled almost thirteen miles that day spanning a period of about six and a half hours. Compared to our normal ride duration at that time, it was about five hours longer than we were used to being in the saddle. Because I struggled so much with remounting, I spent all but a few brief moments in that saddle that day. I think I felt that ride for several days after.

During and after that ride, I came to the realization I needed to seriously correct a few things. First and foremost, I needed to address getting back up on my horse when there is no mounting block. Second, I needed to get in a lot better physical condition or at least get more strength in my legs to remount. And third, lose some weight old man.

Nothing like a few more goals, eh Jerry?

AT THE END OF OUR FIRST full year with our horses I found myself doing some serious self-reflection.

I felt a little more comfortable riding. Of course, my equitation was anything but correct, but then again, I still didn't even know what that meant.

I had been lucky so far, I had not broken anything falling off the horse, unlike Deirdre. Then again, she broke after falling down, not falling off. I wondered, then, if that really qualified as a horse injury.

When I fell off, I wore out a lot of boot leather hiking around as I looked for a very tall log or rock to use as a mounting block. I definitely needed to work on that.

Other than our best friend, Deirdre and I spent the vast majority of our time alone on those horses. Something I would look back on one day with understanding.

But overall life was good, and we were still riding.

As winter settled in, I was looking forward to some nice relaxing time off enjoying the warmth and comfort of my home. I anticipated that we would still be going up to see the horses once or twice a week, but deep down in a hidden cavern in my mind, I knew Deirdre was going to want to go up a touch more than that. But I tried my darndest to ignore that nagging little thought.

Holy Crap

———

THE NICE PART about where we were boarding was that it bordered the forest. When the snow was not too heavy or deep, we would simply tack up and go wander the fields and trails. That was so much more preferrable than working in the run-in. That second winter we were able to ride in the snow often, which in and of itself was good, because we still could not load the horses on the trailer.

We spent the winter once again up at the barn almost every evening and every day off, basically any chance we had. I'm not sure why I never noticed the mud the first winter. Maybe it was because we came up after turn-in more often, or they were in the run in when we got there. But, by February of the second winter, after making countless trips into the sacrifice pasture to retrieve the horses, I noticed.

Just being me, I decided to do a little research on all that mud.

There were six horses at our facility sharing a one-acre winter sacrifice pasture. There was a thirty-foot area along the inside of the fence line that was a bit more solid, as solid as is possible in a sacrifice pasture, but the closer you got to the round bale feeder the deeper, mushier and more treacherous the mud became. That soft, boot sucking, fall causing, deep brown viscous looking mud soup intrigued me.

Online I went, searching for information about the average output of a horse.

Did you know: *"Manure includes both the solid and liquid portions of waste. Horse manure is about 60 percent solids and 40 percent urine. On average, a horse produces 0.5 ounce of feces and 0.3 fluid ounce of urine per pound of body weight every day. A 1,000-pound horse produces about*

31 pounds of feces and 2.4 gallons of urine daily, which totals around 51 pounds of total raw waste per day." (2)

After finding that little nugget of information I started to do some simple math.

If six horses are kept exclusively in a one-acre area from November 1st until April 15th (166 days) and each horse produces approximately fifty pounds of raw waste per day, how much raw waste is in the winter pasture at the end of winter?

Taking into consideration that the horses spend an average of sixteen hours a day outside and eight hours a day in their stalls, we can safely conclude that approximately 67%, or 33.5 pounds of their raw waste will be delivered outside.

Therefore, six horses will deposit approximately 201 pounds of waste per day outside.

There are 166 days between November 1st and April 15th.

If my calculations are anywhere near accurate, here is what the formula my simple mind came up with:

166 x 201 = 33,366 pounds or 16.6 tons of raw waste is excreted by the horses in that one-acre sacrifice pasture over the winter.

As to the horses eating habits, we can safely assume that the horse, while in the sacrifice pasture, will spend approximately 75% of their day eating from the round bale feeder.

I figure that 75% of the raw waste will most likely be accumulated around that feeder.

Thus, my theory is:

FROM MY SADDLE LIFE IS A GREAT ADVENTURE

On April 14th when I walk out to get my horse from the round bale feeder, I will have to successfully maneuver through about 12.4 tons of horse manure.

And to think we still call it mud.

Testing The Waters

T HAT SPRING, Deirdre signed up for a three-day beginner's horsemanship clinic at a local facility. As for me? I felt I was becoming more and more comfortable on Montana, so the thought of taking a "class" for something I was doing just fine on my own was totally out of the question.

My attitude toward improving my skill through lessons was a holdover from a poor experience I had back in my twenties. Forty some years ago, I had been steadily improving my golf game, dropping strokes regularly and scoring in the mid-nineties. For an amateur duffer, I was happy and enjoying the game. Then my ex-father-in-law convinced me to take some lessons to help improve my game, so I did. I have not scored a round under one hundred and ten since. If and when I play golf these days, I have three steadfast rules: 1- A twelve pack for every nine holes. 2 – Absolutely no score cards anywhere. 3 – If I pick up the ball and throw it while cussing bothers you, we shouldn't probably play golf together.

No sir. I can handle learning to ride on my own just fine, thank you very much. I happily audited the clinic while I took like seven hundred pictures of everyone during those three days. I listened to what the clinician was teaching, but I didn't really understand a single thing he was talking about. It didn't matter to me anyway, though, because I knew Deirdre would explain it all to me later.

Even though I did not understand what he meant when he said, "lean back, tighten your core, don't squeeze, hands forward", I did find myself trying to see what the riders were doing. Of course, what I thought I saw and what he meant were on two different planets.

On the second evening, the clinician helped us load Montana on the trailer. There is something about that fabled 'Appaloosa strong will' that will make you laugh and cry. It was a difficult process right out of the chute, and for a time I didn't think the clinician was going to win. There were a lot of walk ups to the trailer and back aways, tight lunge circles and steps in and steps out of the trailer. Then the clinician took off his vest after about twenty minutes of hard, sweaty work for both man and beast. It was time for things to get serious. In no time at all, he had Montana self-loading like she had been doing it her whole life.

Ahhhh, now if we could just do that too! He worked with Deirdre the next day, and before we took Montana home, we were loading her in and out of the trailer just fine.

As it turned out, Deirdre learned quite a bit from that clinic. We started trying some of the different things she had learned during our rides. We still did not have or understand the proper techniques yet but at least we had something. We kept on experimenting. The really cool thing was we were now able to get Montana on the trailer.

We were excited that we were able to finally load the horses but unfortunately, we had no idea where to go, so we didn't haul out anywhere. No one was knocking down our door to go ride with them, so we were fortunate we still had the whole forest at our back door. We did haul out and ride a couple of large, organized fundraisers but for the most part we just stuck around in our little neck of the woods. We made sure to load the horses on and off the trailer regularly though, even take them for short rides in the trailer, just in case someone called and asked, "Hey, want to join us?"

Long about mid-summer, we got our first personal invitation to haul out to a trailhead and ride. Well, it would technically have been our second invitation, but I chose to forget about my first loading fiasco. We were so excited to go and meet our waitress friend to ride a trail system just over the border in New York. We were finally going to ride our horses just like all the real horse people do. WaHooooo!

The ride was not very long or very difficult, but it was new. The trails were fairly easy compared to our woods around the barn and we did have a map, sort of. Part of the trail system included an old, closed ski resort Deirdre and I had frequented many years ago as downhillers. It was so cool riding on the old cross-country trails and ski slopes we used to ski on during winter months. We rode around the old lifts on the top and bottom of the slopes, and by the old loading huts. We even got to cross our first wooden bridge. Actually, we couldn't get our horses to cross it while in the saddle, so we had to get down and lead them across. That was okay, though, because we were finally getting better at finding something to stand on to mount.

Life that day was incredibly awesome.

Them Bones, Them Bones

W E HAULED OUT several more times after that before I would learn a valuable lesson about tacking up my horse.

Tacking a horse looks so simple when you watch westerns on TV. The cowboy just throws a saddle up on a horse, pulls a leather strap on the side, ties down his saddle bags, swings himself up into the saddle and rides away. Seriously, have you ever seen them check for proper fit? Have you ever seen them securing a breast collar? How about securing the front and rear cinches. Have you noticed in the movies the horses are always bridled and ready and never have a halter on when it's time to tack up? Although it is not hard tacking up, it is still a little more than wham bam, thank you ma'am.

It was going to be a stunning July day and Deirdre had to work. I called my brother and he readily agreed to come ride Montana with me in the woods around the barn. We were both excitedly looking forward to spending some time together on the horses. After helping him tack Montana, I set to work tacking Jesse. Excited and anxious to get riding, I hurried right along tacking up my horse so we could get underway. He mounted Montana and I waited until he was settled in then I brought Jesse to the block.

My mounting technique had improved significantly since that first fiasco on Montana. From the mounting block, I slipped my foot into the stirrup with my reins in my left hand holding the horn and my right hand on the cantle. Up I went and down in the saddle I sat. Adjusted my seat a little to get comfortable and asked Jesse to walk out.

Suddenly, it was like I just left the chute and had to hang on until the eight second horn.

Eight seconds? I didn't even last two seconds. I went flying through the air and hit the ground with a thud. A little dazed and confused, I just sat there on the ground. I realized that I was still able to move and breath. Well, okay then.

I got up and started brushing myself off looking for Jesse. Then this thought slowly started to creep into my head and began to repeat itself over and over, and it was not, "What the hell just happened?"

It was a line from some song that went something like, "Every time I fall, I get back up again." (3)

Without consciously realizing it, I was determined to get back up on that horse. It was not like I had not fallen off and gotten back up more times than I could count already in my riding career. This time getting back up just felt, different. Never mind the obvious first question I should have been asking; "What made her do that?"

Jesse was peacefully eating grass, a couple feet away and never flinched as I walked up and retrieved her for another round. I kind of lectured her with a "what was that all about" conversation as I led her back to the mounting block and proceeded to set her up to mount again.

Now at that point, common sense should have reached out and slapped me so hard upside my head it would have made my ears ring. Why I never once thought, "What just happened was so out of character for Jesse. Is there something wrong?" I do not know. I most certainly should have.

Instead, I was laser focused on one thing. Getting back up on that horse. All I kept hearing in my simple head was, "If you fall, get back up again."

Same routine. I got up. I sat down. I settled in and adjusted. I asked her to step out. Once again, I didn't make it two seconds before I went flying through the air and hit the ground.

This time I hit the ground hard enough to make the record skip. I felt that landing. I struggled trying to get back up. My brother had already dismounted and was standing over me helping me up and asking if I was okay. I slowly worked my way up off the ground, struggling to breathe or to even move for that matter, but I was moving. Ignoring the pain, I bullheadedly concluded nothing was broken other than my pride.

The volume of that verse now in my head was up to ten, blasting in my skull. I could hear it screaming, "EVERY TIME I FALL, I GET BACK UP AGAIN".

How does that definition of insanity go? "Repeating the same thing over and over expecting different results?"

I had just gathered up Jesse for round three, when the owner of the barn showed up to check on all the commotion. I gave him a quick rundown as I was squaring Jesse up to the block. The two of them must have seen something I didn't, because they both diligently tried to convince me not to get back up. But this Ca'boy was having none of that because I all I could hear was "EVERY TIME I FALL, I GET BACK UP AGAIN,"

My brother held Jesse for me as I once again, this time very slowly, climbed the mounting block. I took the reins in my hand and placed my foot in the stirrup. The moment I started to step up, my body let me know this was not a good idea. I bent over Jesse in pain as all the air in my lungs escaped. There was no way I was getting back on that horse, regardless of what that stupid voice in my head was singing.

My brother helped me sit down on the mounting block and the two of them un-tacked the horses and put them back out to pasture. By the time they were done, I was sort of breathing normally again and the pain was bearable. My brother helped me into the truck and asked if I wanted to go to the hospital. I told him I didn't, I just wanted to go home and sit for a while. Once I was in the truck and it started to move, there was no doubt in my mind I was really going to feel this in the morning.

When we arrived at the house, it took some effort to get up the porch steps and inside where I opted to sit in my computer chair. It was higher with a more rigid back. I knew I would not be able to get up off the sofa or out of the recliner once I had sunk down into either one of them.

For the next hour or so we just sat there, as my brother chuckled while repeatedly telling me how funny I looked flying through the air before landing with a thud like a big turd. If you have a sibling, you know the rules. Mercilessly bust on the one that is hurt because they were the one stupid enough to get hurt. We are your typical brothers, always laughing at the others' pain.

It was all humor and jokes until I had to go to the bathroom. I started to get up from my chair and the pain took my breath away. I had my brother help me up, I stood for a second and had to sit back down. I could barely walk or breathe. Once I caught my breath, he helped me up again with the same results.

"I think maybe you should take me to the hospital, bro."

After what seemed like hours of slow painful maneuvering to the bathroom, out of the house and down the steps, I was finally in the truck and ER bound. My wife is an RN at the hospital where I was headed. Through the pain and labored breathing, I had enough sense to send her a text message telling her I was coming to visit her fine establishment. Best let her know before I just showed up and they called her from the ER. Funny how wives get when you don't tell them certain things.

"If you fall," you get five fractured ribs and you don't "Get back up again," because you spend two days in the ICU and the next several weeks recovering. I figured out that you EVENTUALLY get back up again, but not necessarily right after you fall. Amazingly, I still like that stupid song.

As much as I would love to brag about how I cowboyed up and pushed through the pain, that I pushed through the lack of sleep, that I fought my heart out to get moving again so I could get out of that hospital and go home and ride my horse, I cannot. I did it because of my butt. That's right, my butt.

I tolerated a nurse helping me twice and that was it. No more. End of line. The third time I had to go, I had them help me into the bathroom. I absolutely was not going to let someone do that for me again. I swear I would have died in that little six by six cubicle sitting on that porcelain throne before another nurse touched my butt with a Sani-wipe. It took me quite a while to figure it out and it hurt like hell, but I did it myself from then on.

Oh yeah, I almost forgot about that tacking up thing I mentioned. Once I was able to move and get around a little and head back up to the barn, I talked to the barn owner. Seems when he untacked Jesse, he found the rear cinch connector strap was not secured forward on the front cinch. He suspected when I asked her to move out, the rear cinch came up under her and suddenly acted like a bucking strap. No kidding. Who knew?

That was a life lesson that I will never forget.

Horses and Camping

———

MY SISTER WANTED TO COME UP from Florida with her horses and ride with us. She has been riding since she was young and has had horses most of her adult life. The facility where we purchased Jesse is also a well-known riding destination with hundreds of miles of trails, stalls, campsites, and cabins. A plan was formulated. She would rent a cabin and we would pull our camper down and spend ten days together that fall.

There was a special event for the first five days at camp offering two guided group rides per day to choose from along with clinics, demonstrations and games such as ranch sorting. There was a huge cowboy buffet each night for dinner and a big tack auction the last day. The event also featured a nationally known clinician (my sister's all-time favorite, I would learn) who gave demonstrations, lectures and offered small group townhall type question/answer sessions.

We had absolutely no clue how any of that stuff worked, but we were all in anyway. We just had to decide which guided group trail ride we wanted to go on each day and let the adventures begin.

On our first day of riding, we opted for the long day ride down and across the river. The day began by loading the horses onto a stock trailer at the campground and hauling them to the trailhead. Leaving the trailhead, we would ride to the river, cross over and head up into the forest on the other side. We would stop for lunch and cross the river in another location, then proceed back to our pickup point at a little general store.

That first ride was an eye opener on several levels for me. It started out with loading Montana onto a huge stock trailer. Now who would have thought Montana and loading could possibly be an issue?

As we waited our turn, I watched the trail boss loading the first trailer. His M.O. was to grab the horses lead rope and pull them into the trailer. I was pretty certain Montana was not going to take that too well. Once the first trailer was loaded and gone, Jesse was the first to load on the next trailer. Then it was Montana's turn. I stepped up and handed the trail boss her lead. I mentioned to him he may not want to yank the lead, or she may refuse to get on.

I squarely got that "This is not my first rodeo" look from him as he took the lead from my hand and immediately gave it a good hard tug while still looking me squarely in the eye. In her true Appaloosa form, Montana immediately planted her feet, raised her head, and proceeded to yank him right out of the trailer before he knew it was coming. As much as I was concerned, I also thought it was funny. I had warned him.

We had just spent over a year figuring this out, and now in less than fifteen seconds some cowboy who thought his crap didn't stink may have just set us back to square one. Then I saw that look in his eyes. Sheer determination to dominate any horse that dared to defy him. It was quickly going to get damn interesting. My money was on the horse.

He proceeded to give her a couple of downright definitive hard tugs on the lead rope. She responded by backing further across the parking lot hauling him right along with her. To his credit once she stopped, he waited a few seconds until she calmed a touch then he gently led her back to the trailer and stepped back inside. Montana walked up to the door and came to an abrupt stop. He gave a hard tug and pulled. I watched the instant replay, as once again Montana pulled him out of the trailer. Only this time she just kept on going and took him thirty-feet across the parking lot.

This whole process recycled itself maybe three or four times until the he looked at me and said, "If the horse won't load looks like you're not going."

Deep down inside, as much as I enjoyed watching Montana put that arrogant son-of-a-buck in his place, I was concerned, and my heart was pounding in my chest. I had no experience with anything like this. I had no idea whatsoever how to solve this problem. On top of all that I was there with three other members of my family waiting to take the first trail ride of our vacation. Nothing like feeling some pressure at eight o'clock in the morning.

I asked the trail boss if I could try. I mean what did I have to lose, right? If she didn't load, I didn't go, which was pretty much where we currently were anyway. If she did load, I got to go, which was the preferable outcome.

He handed me the lead with a flare of the dramatic and stepped away. I walked up to my horse and rubbed her jowl and looked her in the eye. We stood there for a brief second or two and after I recited the "Alan Sheppard" prayer in my head, I started for the trailer with her a half a step behind me on a loose lead. I stepped into the trailer, turned just enough to catch her in my peripheral vison and kept walking, making sure not to apply any pressure on the lead.

It was the moment of truth. Will she, or won't she?

Looking straight forward into the trailer I walked slowly and calmly. Then I heard the first hoof step up quickly followed by the other three. The next thing I knew I was tying her off next to Jesse. Man did I love on that horse. It is said they can feel heart rates. If that is true then while my arms were hugging her neck, she not only felt my heart she accessed my soul.

The trail boss did not acknowledge what had just happened, nor did it really matter, we were loaded. Something told me that admitting defeat would never work for him anyway. So, on my way past him as I exited the trailer, I chuckled loud enough so he could hear me without even glancing in his direction, simply because I just plain wanted to.

That was absolutely the first time I accomplished exactly what I wanted to with my horse. It was a beginning way before I began my horsemanship journey, and a huge accomplishment for me at the time.

Crossing the river would be the next eye-opening event for me on that ride. To date we had done some very small stream crossings and even walked down a stream, but this was a river.

Before we left the trailhead where everyone unloaded, the trail boss gave us an overview of the ride ahead. He explained that it was important that we all follow right in his path as we crossed the river. If we wandered too far up or down stream, we could step into unseen deep holes.

When we rode out, we found ourselves about two thirds of the way back in the group of about twenty-five riders. We rode some forest trails for a fair amount of time before we exited the woods and I saw the river for the first time. My first thought was, "That's a big river."

As we worked our way slowly toward the entry point, I watched as the first riders started to cross. I estimated we would be crossing about two-hundred feet of water, about three feet deep. By the time we reached the water, the trail boss was almost ready to exit on the far side. The line of riders ahead of me looked like a lazy snake slithering over the water as we prepared to follow the riders in front of us into the river.

When our moment came to start across the river, there could be no hesitation. My sister, who was in front of us, was shouting instructions to Deirdre and me. At the time I am sure I heard them, and they probably even made sense somewhere in my excited brain as I asked Montana to step into the water. I will never forget the look of thrill on Deirdre's face and hearing her excited giggle.

It was a big first for us. I was initially a little nervous about crossing but not afraid. When you are part of a group who are successfully doing what you will soon have to do, your confidence becomes stronger and replaces your fear. Watching all those other riders out there crossing that river with no issues made it easier for me to be confident that I could do the same.

It would be another year before I would meet the trainer who has helped transform my horsemanship. One of the many 'catch phrases' she has is: "Never confuse confidence with competence." Once I heard it for the first time, it would take a while before it would truly make sense to me, but on that day as I stepped into that river it was truly all about my confidence to successfully cross that river.

Once the river crossing was behind us, we made our way up into the mountains and forest trails on the other side. That is where the next eye-opening event would occur: bees.

I have no idea where, when, what or how many but I do remember hearing someone yell "BEES" and my sister screaming from behind me, "RUN, ROD, RUN."

Are you kidding me? RUN? My God, I can barely stay on this horse walking. I was just beginning to dabble in a little trotting and now you want me to run.

WHOA, SHUT THE FRONT DOOR.

"DAMN IT ROD, RUN," my sister screamed again from behind me. I quickly found out that I had absolutely no choice in the matter. The riders both in front and behind me were starting to canter, which in turn sent the signal to Montana that she needed to canter as well. A split second later we were hauling out across the forest at warp-10.

The only thing that was going through my head was survival. I had absolutely no clue how to ride at this speed. I had really no clue how to ride at any speed, but I held on to that horse with every part of my body I could hang on with. I was running down that trail like a fighter jet getting launched from an aircraft carrier.

Then I saw it. Eye-opener number four. There was a fallen tree across the trail.

I was going to die. I was going to go flying off this horse and die. A two-foot diameter tree that I could have easily stepped over at a walk. Instead, I was about to go over it while traveling a zillion miles per hour.

Adios and vaya con dios, Rod.

As fast as it began it was over. I was still in the saddle and the bees and tree were behind us. I heard people yelling slow down. Ahhhhh. Okay. HOW?

Thank God for tolerant horses. I did the only thing I could think of to stop. I pulled her face and jaw up and back as hard as I could. To her credit Montana slowed right down and just pulled her reins back down out of my death grip. Oh, my Lord, that poor horse.

I took quick stock of myself to confirm that I was in fact still alive and not some aberration floating around. My heart was racing, my body was shaking, and my wife was laughing hysterically. Deirdre was laughing. That only meant one thing. A situation like that, as scary as it was, she loved it. As for me? Maybe not so much.

We finished the rest of that ride with no more eye openers. We were soon waiting at a general store for the stock trailers to show up to take us back to camp. This time when the same trail boss asked for Montana's lead, I just walked past him with my horse and loaded her myself. Thank you very much but, no thanks. The memories of that first ride will live with me forever.

My first trot on Jesse would also become an unforgettable memory while we were on that vacation. I had ridden Jesse several times before, but always at a walk. Montana has the smoothest trot in the world. No bounce, no post, no work. Jesse, as I would find out, was a tad bit different.

My brother and his wife, our best friends and friends of my sisters had stopped down to visit one day, and we decided to take a short ride on the trails around the campground that evening after dinner. Deirdre offered to stay behind so our guests could ride so ended up riding Jesse. Our little group headed out with my sister on point and me on drag. We started up a small incline on the trail and everyone in front of me decided to step up into a trot. The word "post" had a few definitions for me at that point in my life. Post a sign, post in the ground, post a letter, post haste, Post cereal but I didn't recollect one that involved horses.

I set all the gears in motion for Jesse to trot, which really was nothing more than letting her follow the other horses. I was so used to Montana that I never thought about Jesse riding any differently. Silly me. I felt that little collection before the transition. I sat down comfortably in the saddle like I did with Montana. Then she stepped up into her trot and out of the saddle I went. Her back dropped away, and my butt stayed suspended there for a nano second. Then my butt started down as her back was coming up.

The saddle and I met somewhere in between. It was a white light and breath-taking kind of contact. Then we did it a second time. You can rest assured we did not do it a third time. By the time I got back to camp, I was not even sure I was going to be able to get off the horse. When I finally was able to dismount, my knees buckled from the pain in my lower back and took the breath out of me. Pain and not breathing, a feeling I was starting to become accustomed to it seemed.

We were only about halfway through our vacation. As much as I hurt, I knew I still had to ride. My wife, the ever-ready nurse, fed me some Tylenol then my brother-in-law suggested he and I make the thirty-minute trip to town to find a lower back brace. The brace helped just enough to let me ride and I was good to go. I cowboyed up every morning and rode the rest of that vacation, but I barely moved from my camp chair the rest of the time. It wouldn't be until my next trip to the ER that I would learn why my back hurt so much.

On that trip I would come to several realizations. One of the more outstanding things was that I was not as great of a map / GPS reader as I believed myself to be. I was definitely still overweight and needed to continue losing weight as well as becoming more committed in the physical conditioning department. Traveling with horses was not all just ride then kick back, eat and drink. Those suckers required a lot of attention.

Although I could easily share several more daily adventures about our first overnight trip with the horses, I will move on to other memories leaving this chapter in my horsemanship journey behind us. On a huge positive note as we depart this chapter, the greatest thing that came of it was that from this point on, we would find ourselves hauling out more and more.

RN Sí Vet Tech No

ROLLING INTO OUR THIRD year of riding, it was starting to feel like all the time we had spent with the horses was beginning to pay off. That basically means we did not seem to be falling off as often. We were experimenting with more trotting, mostly while going up inclines, but we still walked most of the time. It seemed like we were finally moving forward. I started to feel like Montana and I were beginning to form a mutual understanding with each other. The time spent with my sister helped a lot. She imparted a lot of useful tips and pointers that were helping me along the way. But to be honest, at the end of the day I still kicked to go, pulled to stop, and yanked to turn.

We were also hauling out and riding new trail systems with our friends more often. It wasn't long before Deirdre and I began loading up the girls and hauling them out on our own to ride. It was such a rewarding experience for the two of us. She and I spent most of our time on the horses alone, so being able to leave our comfort zone around the barn and challenge new trails was an incredible high for us.

Not to underscore the trails around the barn. mind you. They were, and still are, incredible trails. Seriously, from our back door we were in the National Forest within ten minutes. We started to wander out for two or three hours at a time. We could cover as many miles as we were willing to ride. Once we became familiar with new trails in the forest, we started to ride them and explore. We certainly spent our fair share of time lost, which also taught us more about navigating in the wilderness. Indeed, those trails we called our comfort zone were rather challenging at times as well. Sort of a win, win you might say.

All the hours the two of us spent out there riding behind the barn in those woods, weaving trees, learning how to turn, (using only the reins, grrrr) how to step over logs, cross streams, trot and stay on. I believe all of that is why, to this day, we have such a deep, profound love of trail riding. The time we spent in our comfort zone around that barn taught us that we could be adventurous and exploring "Trail Riders."

That summer started out to be the most active trail riding we had done so far, right up until one afternoon in August.

We were riding out of the barn on our way to the forest. We had just passed the winter pasture when a grouse, pheasant, woodchuck, or something suddenly made a huge commotion in the scrub to our right, spooking both horses. It never came into view but both horses immediately dipped and jumped sideways spinning their shoulders, ready to run away from the sound. Deirdre came off but by some miracle I stayed on. Deirdre, Montana, and I were all fine but for just a little elevation in heart rate. Jesse, however, didn't fare so well.

We quickly noticed a huge gash on the back of her leg above her right front fetlock. It was about an inch or two wide running from one side of the leg to the other exposing the tendon. We now had our first major medical experience associated with horses. Thankfully, we were still very close to the barn. We returned and rinsed the wound and lightly covered it as we reached out to our vet for help. Unbelievably, and thankfully, the vet was there in under an hour.

Once the vet arrived, he got right to it and had her all prepped and ready for sutures in no time. Now enter Deirdre the Registered Nurse that deals with wounds and surgeries all the time. She loves watching surgery on TV and the ER emergency room shows. This was going to be right up her alley.

As for me? I can't stand that stuff. I do not want to know what they are going to do to me. No, not at all. When she watches that stuff, I leave the room and go do anything else. Once she wanted to watch a knee replacement, so I went in the next room to do some computer work. I was okay hearing the muffled words from the TV as I worked away. Then I heard the drill. I know what a cordless drill sounds like. I went and cleaned the garage.

Don't get me wrong, I can handle that stuff if necessary. I'm not squeamish in an emergency, but to choose to see it, nah. So now here we are with a big, huge gash, tendons exposed and a vet that will need a hand as he sutures the horse. I was so lucky to have Deirdre there to help the vet.

She had been holding Jesse's head while I held up the leg so the vet could flush it and prep it for sutures. Here comes the best part of this memory.

"Can you just keep holding the leg up while I suture?" the vet asked. I turned and looked for Deirdre to take over because I was sure she would want to get involved in this part. She didn't move.

"Hon, you want to get down here and do this?" I asked, offering her the opportunity to change places. This girl would watch open heart surgery from the gallery if she had a chance.

"No, it's okay." I just looked at her with a blank stare. She just stood there, motionless holding Jesse's head.

"Are you sure? I thought you would want to see this."

"No, that's okay." What? I literally did not know what to say. I mean I just had no words.

I bent back down and lifted up Jesse's leg once again and proceeded to help the vet. Like I said, I'm not squeamish when the situation calls for me to be involved. Obviously being up close and personal with the vet was suddenly squarely in my wheelhouse. He explained what he needed me to do and got to work. He was really good at explaining everything as he was working, and I actually found it interesting. I didn't understand some of his big words & terminology, but it was pretty easy to understand what he meant by watching as he did it.

For the most part I held up pretty good until he put the first suture in. I was holding Jesse's leg and foot up on my leg to stabilize it for him as he explained how the hooked suture needle worked. Then he proceeded to pass it through the hide. I'm not sure if I heard it or felt it in her leg, but there was a pop as the needle went through the hide. I was all good with everything else up to that point but for some reason that took me by surprise. Not wanting to contaminate the wound by showing everyone what I had for lunch that day, I quickly turned my face away, took a couple deep breaths and shook my head to clear it while making sure I continued to hold the leg and foot stable. Then I got back to my job. After the third suture it wasn't so bad. I even watched more closely as he showed me how he tied off the sutures and cut them off.

Thanks Hon. I would have been just fine not doing that.

After he was done tending to Jesse's immediate situation, he suggested that we take her to another vet more specialized in that type of wound. He was concerned about infection with the tendon being exposed and thought it would be best to take her elsewhere for specialized care. We agreed, and while he was still on-site, he made arrangements for us to transport her the next day.

Curiosity is a strange thing, but bewilderment can be even stranger. I thought I knew my wife fairly well until she simply did not want to help the vet. I had to ask. So, on our way home that evening I did.

Apparently, she has a hard time dealing with injuries to her pets. Okay, I sort of understood, I guess. I recalled her being intrigued several years ago when I was in the hospital, and they had considerable difficulty removing the dressing from my leg wound. Jesse's leg was much easier to deal with then that had been. Well at least she doesn't think of me as a pet. That's a good thing, right?

Jesse was laid up for a bit, but she healed up just fine and we were soon back on the trails.

Deirdre attended her second three-day clinic in the fall of that year, while I still just sat on the sideline and audited parts of it. The old golf lesson theory was still laser focused in my mind. Deirdre enjoyed her clinic and once again I waited for her to impart all her newfound knowledge to me when we were back out in the woods trail riding.

It was during that clinic that we started getting to know our trainer. The clinician also began to play a very important role in our advancement as well. He would soon teach us we could step outside of our comfort zone and push the envelope while still respecting our fear.

During a lunch break one afternoon while I was auditing, our trainer asked me why I was not attending the clinic. My golfer alter ego just jumped right in without a second's hesitation. "I don't need lessons or clinics; I'm doing fine on my own."

I find humor these days when she subtly reminds me of that conversation. Typically, the reminder will pop-up when I am being a little 'resistant' to input as I am struggling with something. I cannot think of a time when she offered advice that I have not stopped, taken a breath, and listened. It didn't matter what I was working on, a smoother transition, lead departure, softening the horse or any one of a zillion other things, she has always helped me over the years. That one silly reminder always brings me back to reality, and I listen.

A New Home

―――

THE DYNAMICS AT OUR STABLE were changing and it was going to require us to relocate the horses. The two clinics Deirdre had taken were at a beautiful facility in the area, so we reached out to them to check on possible boarding opportunities. Fortunately, there were available stalls, so we relocated the girls in December to their new home.

On the downside, we lost the easy access to the forest from the barn and all the beautiful trails it afforded. On the upside, we gained a huge indoor and outdoor arena, better pastures, and a professional facility. The indoor arena meant we would be able to ride more in the winter. We knew going in that the relocation would require significantly more hauling out to ride trails, but we were okay with that. Change is always difficult and even more so when you are not very knowledgeable. As much as we did not want to leave where we were, ultimately it would work out for the best.

It was three days after Christmas and the horses seemed well settled in their new home. It was time for us to check out the new arena opportunities. The sun was slowly beginning to rise in the morning sky, and we were giddy with excitement as we drove the fifteen minutes to the barn. We excitedly jabbered back and forth about how awesome the one hundred by two-hundred-foot arena was going to be compared to the small run-in we had left behind. We just could not wait to saddle up and try it out.

We collected the horses and quickly got them groomed and tacked and led them into the beautiful, indoor arena that we had all to ourselves. OMG we were about ready to wet ourselves as we mounted up and started to ride. Inside. In the winter. One of the advantages of being old is you get up when you used to go to bed, and not many folks are up moving at eight-thirty in the morning.

We slowly circled the arena, riding side by side along the rail. It felt so good to be on the horses inside while it was snowing outside. We cut across the arena just letting the girls walk aimlessly as we just enjoyed the feel of being in the saddle in that huge indoor space.

I believe it was maybe five minutes before I asked Deirdre, "Now what do we do?"

For three years we had been stuck in the black hole of self-teaching. Weaving trees. Trail ride experimenting. Trying not to fall off. Now here we were with all the room in the world, and we had no clue what to do in that beautiful arena.

In the woods there was always something. A tree, a log, a turn, a hill, a spook, a trail to look for, a map to follow, a stream to cross, a new trail to explore. There was always something. We never had to think about what we wanted to do, because the trail and woods provided all of the obstacles and challenges for us. And we could do it all at a walk or sometimes a trot. God, forbid we cantered. NOT CANTER. No, No, NO.

After ten minutes we both concluded that the arena was the most boring, unproductive, unsafe place in the world to ride your horse and we were bored stupid...

Oh my! How things would change down the road.

We didn't give up on the arena. The rest of that winter we did our due diligence and forced ourselves to spend time in that arena just to be on the horses. We were bored out of our skulls as we walked around aimlessly for about half an hour until we could not take it anymore. But it was there, so we forced ourselves to use it. One day down the road, we would discover that the arena would play a huge part in advancing our horsemanship. But it absolutely was not that winter.

Shaken not Stirred.

———

A S WE ROLLED INTO SPRING, one of our fellow boarders
introduced us to a small, wooded area close to the barn where we
were allowed to ride. To Deirdre and me that was like being given the
keys to the kingdom. It was nothing like riding out of our old barn into
the National Forest, but it was woods, with trees and trails and no need
to haul out. Short one-hour rides in the woods became reality once
again.

Even with that small, wooded area we ultimately hauled out to ride
much more than we rode around the stable. With each trip we became
more and more comfortable with loading the horses onto the trailer
and discovering different places to ride.

It was a beautiful early April day as we started into our fourth riding
season. We had just returned home from an exciting ride on one of the
local trail systems. We were chilling out, relaxing on our front porch,
cheerfully reminiscing about the day. The ride had been a lot of fun and
without incident.

We were languishing in that euphoric feeling you get from a great ride
and rather quickly found ourselves celebrating with a couple of chilled
vodka martinis. Up, slightly dirty, one with a lemon wedge and one
with three olives, thank you very much.

As we relaxed on the porch talking about many things as one topic led
to another. After our second cocktail, we started talking about the time
my sister had come up for a week of riding. As the alcohol flowed so did
our thoughts. Soon we were discussing my sisters' recent purchase of a
living quarters horse trailer (LQ) and traveling with her friends on new,

far away adventures. That coming July, she was heading up to North Carolina and the Great Smoky Mountains with her friends.

Then we had the third martini.

While enjoying the calming effects of my vodka martini, I asked Deirdre what she thought about looking into the possibility of an LQ and seeing if we could surprise my sister and meet her in NC.

My wife and I are well suited to each other. Really, we are. I am methodically organized she is sloppy organized. I fret and worry about the details; she doesn't sweat them at all. When I think the world is going to end, she thinks well let's go out happy partying. But neither one of us has ever, and never will I suspect, say to the other, "Maybe we should give this more thought" when either of us comes up with an idea that sounds like fun. Especially after a couple of toddies.

Tequila. Vodka. Beer. I believe we may be seeing a trend developing here. Look out Bryson City, North Cackalacky, there are going to be some new riders heading your way!

First we found a truck, then we found the LQ. That was probably not done in the proper order, but then again, what did we know? We would learn, one way or the other. Then we called my sister and told her what we had done. By the end of April, we were booked and started planning our first big haul out with our new horse trailer. Wahooo!

We had to get the new trailer stocked and ready. We also had a twenty-eight-foot camper, so we could have just transferred all the necessary utensils from that to the LQ. But as we were still using the camper on a regular basis, we decided to just re-fit the LQ. Then we discovered the lack of storage in the LQ compared to the camper. That was a little bit of an eye opener. Who would have ever thought the LQ was designed to accommodate horses more than humans? But eventually we figured it out and had it ready for use.

We had approximately two months to get everything organized and ready to go, so the research and questions began. We learned that you could use the third stall with the stud wall for storage during the trip, sweet. What we did not learn was that without a hay pod, we needed to use that space to store hay for the horses. But then again, we never even thought about taking that much hay with us at all. We just assumed we could buy it there. We learned one thing and then were taught a bigger lesson.

We did research into how to travel long distances, the time involved and the breaks you needed to provide for the horses. We tapped any resource we could find and, as you might expect, we were more than a little nervous about the trip. We calculated it would take about eleven and a half hours including fuel stops. We would stop every three hours, top off the fuel, and give the horses thirty minutes to relax and drink some water. We planned a layover both down and back, so each day of driving would only be about six or seven hours long. I got a little anal retentive about the horses, so I invested in a trailer cam system so we could see them as we traveled. Great investment. Used once. Willing to sell.

As we continued preparing for the trip, we rode regularly to make sure the girls were in good condition. As we approached our departure date for North Carolina, we prided ourselves on all the trail hours we had accumulated over the last three and a half years, the experiences we had encountered and the obstacles we had overcome out there in the wild rugged forest. We were not falling off nearly as often, and we could even regularly trot up small inclines.

Yes sir-ree bob, we were ready to hit the trails in the Great Smoky's.

On Top of Ole Smoky

———

THE BIG DAY FINALLY ARRIVED. We loaded up the girls and hit the road before the sun was even remotely thinking about rising. Two days later, we safely arrived at our destination.

Now, there are some interesting stories that go along with our layovers. Like backing up a gooseneck for the first time in a tight ninety. That was a brand-new experience I may have wanted to practice at least once before I left. Not like backing up trailers is a common occurrence with horses. Thank goodness the gentleman who owned the facility where we spent the night graciously offered to help us; well, actually, he did it for us. Then when we left, I bottomed out the back end of the trailer and pulled off the rear rubber step guard. Luckily, it was under the tack room door. Or learning the tracking of a three-horse LQ gooseneck down a narrow, tight, winding dirt road was A LOT different than that of a bumper pull. And then there was the sweet tea. Oh My God! If anyone tells you they are from Georgia and offers you sweet tea, the only thing you need to say is, "Please and thank you."

But these are campfire stories I share with our friends while enjoying a nice cold beer. I just cannot do them justice unless I can get my whole body grooving with the story. Uh oh. There's that alcohol again.

Once everyone arrived at the campground and were settled into their sites, we decided our first ride would be out of camp the next day. That first evening, we got the skinny from the campground owner on how things were going to happen. Every morning would start with him coming to our sight to discuss the distance, difficulty, and length of time we would like to ride that day. Once that was determined, he

73

would recommend where we should go and give us a hand drawn map with directions and landmarks to look for.

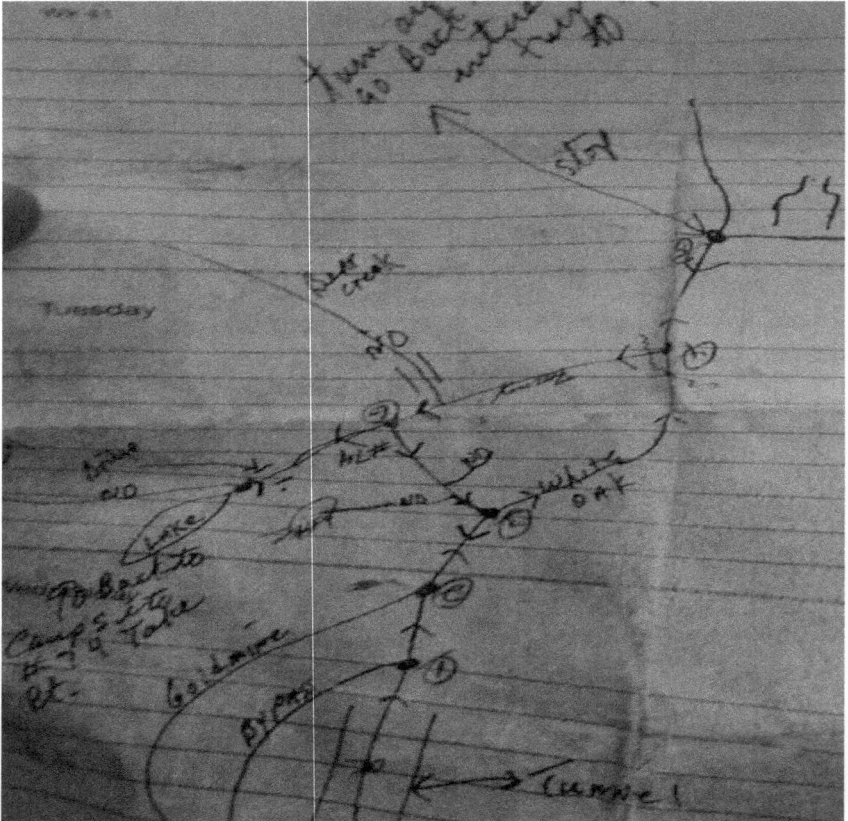

When I started this memoir, I was determined not to use any of the hundreds of thousands of pictures we have taken. But after trying countless times unsuccessfully to explain in writing what those maps looked like, I decided the only way I could do it was with both words and a picture of one of the actual maps.

The picture you just saw is one of the trail maps we used to guide us on our daily rides. They were hand drawn each morning just for us by the campground owner. (Who, by the way, was a retired park trail maintenance engineer.) He explained the direction we were to ride on the trail and the landmarks to look for. Then he told us, if we did happen to get off track, what landmarks we would most likely see to tell us where we were on the map.

After the first planning session, it was apparent that attendance by not just myself, but Deirdre and my sister, was going to be imperative. We would all need to pay close attention to what he was saying. The pencil was drawing and writing on the paper at the same time as the verbal directions were explaining what the pencil was doing. We all sat huddled together at the picnic table, focusing closely as we listened and learned. Then we all took a picture of the day's map. With any luck, between all of us in the group, we would remember all the little details that were imparted to us.

The first ride was nineteen miles, with three gaited horses and our three Quarter Horses. Nothing like breaking out of the gate running. Talk about six hours of fun. Whew. Either we were constantly trying to keep up (remember we were still only moderately strong trotters) or the gaited horses were being held back to stay with us. When the others got too far ahead, they waited patiently for us to catch up. We had already discovered from previous rides at home that it was a rare occasion when gaited and Quarter Horses rode comfortably together. We would have to make some adjustments and/or compromises, or it was going to be a long, hard week for everyone.

That first ride was the longest we had ever ridden, and it was just beautiful. After that first ride, I was certain this was going to be one of the most beautiful places we would ever visit. I also knew, after that ride, we were not going to be able to ride twenty miles a day for the next four days. We had spent significant time in the saddle before the trip to get in shape, but only about three hours per ride. My body made sure it reminded me of that after that first day.

Other than the ride out of camp on the first day, we would use the campgrounds stock trailers to get to the other trailheads, all within reasonable distance. There were five trailers to choose from so, on the first evening, we inspected and chose the trailer we wanted to use during the remainder of the trip.

Our second day we hauled to a trail called "The Road to Nowhere." It was a fourteen-mile ride that started by riding through a tunnel constructed for a road that was never completed. We rode the old, uncompleted road for a short distance until we reached the trail. Then we rode out to an old homestead foundation and fireplace, had lunch, and started the return trip. On the return there was an option of taking the same trail you took out or you could take one or two side trails that would loop out then reconnect to the main trail. We opted for the loop connectors.

Although the ride was five miles less than the day before, it still felt like nineteen at the end of the day. Ughh. It also opened our eyes to what exactly we were getting into on these trails. I started to realize that maybe we weren't as well prepared to ride some of that terrain as I thought. There were plenty of hefty ascents, switchbacks, and descents. The trails, although not narrow, were definitely not wide, either. Finding the sides of the mountains steep on either side of the trail was common.

I found the ascents, though most were switch backs, more difficult following the gaited horses. They just seemed to effortlessly jaunt right up while our horses seemed to struggle. I suspect it was most likely because of our trotting abilities, or lack thereof. We soon agreed to adjust the riding arrangements and have the gaited horses go ahead of us then wait at an appropriate location further up the trail. Once we caught up to them, we would take a break and rest while they would once again ride on ahead. That solved the problem of us trotting to keep up or them holding their horses back. From my perspective, as we were constantly riding on the side of a mountain, the new arrangement had some serious merit.

Who would have thought we would be riding the sides of mountains in the Great Smoky's, right? A good share of the time, there were steep drop offs on either the left or right side of the trail. It was not uncommon to be riding with one stirrup hanging over the side of the mountain with the other millimeters away from touching the bank on the other side. I experienced some harrowing moments on that trip hoping the horse didn't fall off the mountain. I wish I had known about asking for just a little eye on the outside in order to keep the hip away from the cliff. Or that an occasional tap, tap, tap of the outside leg on the barrel would help keep her closer to the wall. But I didn't, so I steered my horse's head away from the cliff with the reins. Where did that put the hip? Hint, not so much where I had hoped. Oh, naivete is such a wonderful thing at times!

There was so much I did not know in general, and so much I did not know about horsemanship. Lucky for me the trails would only get progressively more challenging, and heart stopping, as we rode over the next four days.

On the third day we hauled to ride the Tsali Rec Area System. You want to talk about a mind-numbing trail briefing that morning. Wowsers. On top of the hand drawn map for the day, the mornings briefing also included a 'verbal' explanation, of the "Trail Schedule" for the Tsali Rec Area.

Jan./Feb./March/April/June/Sept./Nov./Dec.

Right Loop and Left Loop:

> *Horses – Tuesday, Thursday, & Saturday*

> *Mountain Bikes –Monday, Wednesday, Friday & Sunday*

Mouse Branch and Thompson Loop:

> *Horses – Monday, Wednesday, Friday, & Sunday*

> *Mountain Bikes – Tuesday, Thursday, & Saturday*

May/July/August/October

Right Loop and Left Loop:

> *Horses – Monday, Wednesday, Friday, & Sunday*

> *Mountain Bikes – Tuesday, Thursday, & Saturday*

Mouse Branch and Thompson Loop:

> *Horses – Tuesday, Thursday, & Saturday*

> *Mountain Bikes – Monday, Wednesday, Friday, & Sunday*
(4)

After that verbal bowl of word soup came the comment: "I believe that the trail loops are also to be traveled clockwise or counterclockwise depending on the day, so today you should go..."

I am still not sure if the "one-way" is really a factual thing or not. I never saw any signs or notices indicating such a thing, but then again, I didn't read all the fine print on the information board at the trail head either.

That third day was going to be a short seven-mile ride on the Thompson Loop. During dinner the night before, we decided we would all haul out together in the morning. When we left the trailhead, however, we would give the gaited group a good ten, or fifteen-minute head start before we rode out. Instead of them waiting for us to catch

78

FROM MY SADDLE LIFE IS A GREAT ADVENTURE

up, they would just enjoy their ride and we would all meet back at camp. That decision not only eliminated a lot of stress for the three of us but for the other riders as well. By the end of day two, Deirdre and I both knew we were riding way out of our league regarding our skill set. We found enough heart thumping moments navigating the trails, so one less item on our plate was a good thing.

On the fourth day, we decided to ride the fourteen-mile Mouse Branch loop out to the Windy Point Overlook. The four miles of trail along the side of the mountain overlooking Fontana Lake on the way to our destination included some of the most breathtaking scenery imaginable. Vistas that took our breath away and trails that made us feel like we were riding in a lush rain forest without the dreaded humidity. But all of that came with a little price tag for us as well.

On that ride I quickly understood why a specifically designated travel direction on the trail would, indeed, be a very smart idea.

We rode some long stretches of very narrow, barely two feet wide sections of trail with probably seventy-degree mountain slopes on each side. It was evident the trails were cut into the mountain side and that they were not natural. There were considerable lengths of trail where, had a hiker been traveling in the opposite direction, they would have had to back track to let us by because there was absolutely no way we could have passed each other. I have no idea what would have happened if it had been another horse and rider.

My thrill-seeking, adrenaline junky sister found that trail the bomb, while Deirdre and I were just hoping to survive it.

As we approached the Windy Point Overlook, we came upon a washed-out section of trail. A tree had been uprooted and tumbled down the side of the mountain taking with it a good amount of the trail, leaving behind a narrow section less than a foot wide and about ten feet long. Our choices were to turn around on the twenty-four-inch-wide trail on which we were currently standing or move forward. We would learn one day that our quarter horses & appaloosa were quite capable of turning on that narrow of a trail, but not that day they weren't.

Forward it was.

"Give them their heads and let them go. Do not look to the side or down, look straight forward." Sound advice from my sister as we proceeded to traverse the section of trail that was taken out by the tree fall.

I know I had my hand forward and gave Montana all the loose rein she could possibly want, but I am pretty sure that what I gave in loose reins I took back in tight legs and sphincter. I was surprised she could even breathe as I tried to flatten a roll of dimes between my butt cheeks. Even as adrenaline charged as I was, I could not help but notice how sure footed my horse was walking that narrow path. Oh, that's right, I was supposed to be looking forward. Right!

We made it across the bad spot in short order, all safe and sound. With my heart settling in my chest, I began to realize that the trail was progressively getting narrower and tighter as we traveled the side of the mountain out to the overlook. Ah yes, that part of the trail where one stirrup would occasionally touch the mountain on one side while the other dangled over the drop off on the other.

After reaching our destination, it was nice to take some time and enjoy the rewards of our labors. It was absolutely beautiful. All too quickly, it seemed, it was time for us to move on. The trail continued around the point for about another mile until it reconnected to the main trail. It appeared to be as narrow and tight as the quarter mile of trail we just rode getting to the point.

After a group discussion, we concluded that even with the washout issue, it might be better to backtrack the short tight section versus a mile or more the other way. I mean, after all, look at our logic. We made it there so we could make it back. We're good.

The Gentleman Ca'boy

O BVIOUSLY, WE SUCCESSFULLY backtracked over the washout and found ourselves once again on a more comfortable trail. I only have one more misguided adventure to share before this particular memory concludes. It involves this gentleman Ca'boy (me) retrieving his pretty Ca'girl's (Deirdre) hat for her.

We were trotting up this little incline when I saw Deirdre's straw hat lift up off her head and float out over the downhill side of the trail landing ever so neatly on top of the scrub. I hollered to stop as I came up alongside the fedora.

"Leave it" I hear my pretty Ca'girl tell me as I was preparing to dismount and retrieve her cover. I understood her frustration with the now disgraced lid, as that was not the first, second or even the third time we had to stop and collect the little rascal.

But I am her Ca'boy. She is my Ca'girl. Ca'boy's always treat their Ca'girl's with dignity and respect. This was my job. It didn't matter that she was momentarily upset at the mischievous bonnet and wanted to leave it there to rot on the side of that mountain. I knew in my heart of hearts the right thing for me to do was to retrieve her hat for her. So, ignoring her disgruntled commands, I prepared to retrieve her hat.

Before dismounting, I did in fact do a survey of my current surroundings. The trail was about three feet wide, and I felt comfortable that I could manage a dismount. Although I knew I was not strong at it, after working as hard as I have been as well as shedding a few pounds, I knew I could ground mount if all else failed. I once again made a final check of the slope on the downhill side. The scrub was thick, but the slope appeared to be rather gradual. That bad little hat was perched just ever so slightly off the trail, and I knew I could get it.

Still ignoring Deirdre's continued scathing lecture about leaving the hat where it was, I proceeded to dismount. As I lowered myself from the saddle, where my right foot was supposed to come in contact with the ground, I suddenly realized there wasn't any ground there. Since I did not stop descending, my left foot soon slipped out of the stirrup. I was expecting to stop on my right foot, so I was not prepared to hold on, and realized I had no grip on my saddle. Still years away from knowing anything about rein management, I had left my lightweight split reins, that were tied in knot, hooked over the horn. I was suddenly a Ca'boy in trouble.

I grabbed at any surrounding scrub within reach to stop my descent down the two-hundred-foot mountainside, when my feet suddenly hit a solid ledge and I came to a stop with my chest level with the trail.

This was a fine predicament, Rod, now what?

I could not climb up the side because there was no footing or handholds to step on or pull myself out with. Crap. Think. I tried to climb out only to confirm what I already knew. That meant one or both girls were going to have to carefully dismount and help me out. Well, so much for coming to my Ca 'girls rescue, now she had to rescue me. I'm not always the brightest bulb on the tree but, if she had to get down and help pull me up, I knew it would come with a significant price tag.

Then I saw it. My left stirrup. I could just reach it and use that to pull myself up and out. Sweet.

I started to reach up, but wait, the hat. It was right there. I quickly grabbed the hat and put it between my teeth.

ROD WELLING

I reached up and took hold of the stirrup when it suddenly dawned on me that I might spook Montana. Not Cool. So as gently as I could, I slowly started to pull and climb at the same time. Then I felt Montana slowly start to walk forward. I was terrified she was going to run off. But no, she added just enough pull to help me crawl up onto the trail on my hands and knees, then she stopped dead.

With hat in hand, I walked up to my horse rubbing her neck and loving on her, thanking her as she just stood there once again giving me that infamous Appy stink eye for my stupidity.

After gallantly returning my Ca 'girls' hat to her, Montana and I wandered a little further up the trail where I found a suitable spot on the uphill side where I offside mounted her for the first time in my life.

Our adventures in the Great Smoky Mountains taught us that sometime naivete is not always a bad thing when it comes to stepping outside your comfort zone. When we look back, we realize the trails and the challenges would not have been as harrowing if we had known then what we know now. None the less, they were still just a bit more than we probably should have taken on with our level of experience.

The trip left us thirsty for more adventures to faraway places that would challenge our resolve and nerve. Plans for our next summer excursion with my sister were already underway as we were preparing to depart North Carolina. Ultimately, that trip to Deep Creek was the beginning of what would become an annual adventure with my sister to ride and explore new and exciting places.

I officially retired in August of that year. The joy and fun associated with horses was getting stronger with every ride. We spent a weekend camping in our LQ with the horses at the campground near us where we had stayed with my sister. We had so much fun while were there, we thought we would buy another horse.

I have no idea why I suggested to my wife just a couple of weeks prior to that weekend that maybe we should look for a third horse, but I did. There was that reasoning we shared. If it sounds cool, let's not think it over, let's just do it. I was not surprised at all when my idea was not rejected.

As the Crow Hops

THERE WAS A TEN-YEAR-OLD paint gelding there on consignment. The consignee had just acquired him a week or so earlier. He explained to us that he had not had a chance to ride him much but told us what he had experienced so far seemed to show a well-behaved and well-mannered horse. The horse apparently came from some folks the consignee knew and they used him as a "grand children" horse. Basically, he was walked and ridden by the kids and was extremely well behaved. All excellent traits for me.

With a couple of years under my belt and a little more knowledge, I felt I was more prepared to buy a horse. I was also buying from the same gentleman who had helped us with Doc'z and Jesse. I was confident he would not intentionally steer us wrong but none the less, this time I actually picked up feet, checked out the tack, walked him and rode him.

When I had the horse stand next to a rock to mount, he asked me why I didn't use the mounting block. I told him it was because there are no mounting blocks on the trail when I need to get back on. He thought about that for a second or two and said, "Damn, your right. I'm going to make sure all the horses I sell from now on will stand next different things to mount."

We walked and trotted around the arena. I still could not canter very well, except in an emergency while holding on to the horn, so no cantering. That little omission would come back to bite me soon enough. The consignee and I left the arena for a short trial ride to make sure I was comfortable with how the horse, and I got along with each other. We returned to the barn, struck a deal, and we now owned another horse.

Once we got him home and settled into his new environment, we brought him into the arena. We rode at a walk and did some short trots for several days, just to get used to him and for him to become used to us. It was during the third or fourth ride when Deirdre asked him for a canter, and we got the first crow hop. At first, we just thought it was something that spooked him, you know like a ray of light, a particle of dust, so she just walked him for a bit then asked and got a nice, short canter out of him.

The next time she rode him and asked for a canter, she got another crow hop. Now questions were starting to form. I walked over and we discussed the situation. We decided to see if there was a possible tack issue, so we checked the tack and found it sound. She rode him out and asked for a canter again and sure enough he crow hopped. After experimenting with this and finding that he would crow hop every time we asked for more than a short trot, we decided to record a video and send it to the consignee and ask his advice. We had a thirty-day guarantee, so we thought it was best to get him up to speed ASAP.

After he watched the video, he thought the horse was just balking when asked to do more work. He told us that we needed to ride through it until he realized crow hopping was not going to get us to stop asking him to step it up. Basically, he thought the horse was lazy and had learned if he crow hopped a little when he didn't like to do something, his rider would stop and dismount. OKAY.

First of all, we were not even remotely skilled enough to know how to "ride through" crow hopping. Second, at the first sign of a potential fall, the first thing we did was pull back and hang on with any part of our body we could, so that was going to be a problem on top of a problem.

But we said OKAY we'll give it a try. We didn't achieve any success in the arena over the next couple of days, so I came up with a brilliant idea.

Let's take him on a ride on the trails near the barn. There is a nice incline that we used while learning how to trot. Maybe if he is with a small herd, he will just think he needs to stay with them and canter okay. So, we put a small group together to try out my theory, and since it was my idea, I would ride the horse. And no, I still did not know how to canter.

We had been on the ride for about thirty minutes and the horse was walking and riding perfectly as we arrived at the incline. I was fourth in the group of five. The first horses started to canter up the incline, then I asked him to canter as well. I thought we were going to do okay for a moment or two until he really started crow hopping.

I don't recall how long I stayed on, but I certainly remember hitting the ground and having the breath knocked out of me. As my head cleared and I desperately tried to get air into my lungs, I heard the rider behind me yelling "RIDER DOWN, RIDER DOWN." By the time I was finally able to get some sort of normal air flow going everyone was there. My brother and wife were off their horses asking if I was okay and trying to help me up.

I sat there just a bit longer catching my breath, trying to figure out how badly I was hurt. I knew I was hurt, just not sure if I had broken anything. I finally reached for my brother's hand to help me stand. As he pulled, I grunted and released his hand like it was a hot iron. I knew instantly that I was broken and that getting up was going to be extremely painful.

I had them pull my saddle and I used it as a back support, so I was able to sit up a little more comfortably. By this time, one of the riders had called 911. Two fire departments were dispatched, and the story has it that a medevac chopper was on standby for "a horseback rider down in the forest." All I knew at the time was I could not move my left arm without excruciating pain and my breathing was extremely strained and hard.

When the firemen arrived and tried to get me on the back board, I thought I was going to pass out. The EMT's and ambulance were waiting about a mile out on the main road. Since I was able to sit and breathe with the saddle as support, they strapped me to my saddle, slid the board under me, lifted me up on the emergency side by side and strapped me down for transport. As a funny side note, I ended up telling the driver which trails to take for the most direct route to the waiting ambulance.

Once we arrived at the ambulance, one of the crew gave me a little something to relieve the pain, and they detached me from my saddle and put me onto a stretcher. As they were about to load me up into the ambulance, I made them hold up so my wife could take off my boots. Don't ask me, I have no idea why I asked for that. Guess I wasn't going out with my boots on that day.

I was not feeling much pain as I laid in the ER and two male nurses started to cut off my shirt and t-shirt. Once those articles were gone, I felt them lift my leg to start cutting off my pants.

"Wait. Those are Duluth pants," the nurse at my head hollers to the nurse getting ready to cut. "I think he would prefer we didn't cut those off." I never thought about it, but since he brought it up, hell yes save them puppies, they aint cheap. So, we saved my Duluth Fire Hose®(5) cargo pants to ride another day.

Once the X-rays were completed and read, I successfully added a fractured shoulder blade and six more fractured ribs to my list of 'Them Bones, Them Bones.' While the ortho doc was going over all my current fractures he asked me when I compressed one of my lower discs. What compressed disc? Then it hit Deirdre and me at the same time. Jesse, two years earlier, on our first painful trot together. Told you earlier, it would be on this visit I would find out why it hurt so bad.

In the first sixty-two years of my life, I had one broken bone. From sixty-two to sixty-five, I accumulated thirteen more and a compressed disc. I guess I wasn't too surprised when my primary doctor ordered a bone density scan, started me on a calcium regimen and suggested I might want to consider bird watching at my age.

Twelve short days after we bought him, our new horse went back to the consignee per his guarantee. I spent the next couple of weeks healing. Four weeks later I was back up on Montana doing easy arena riding and five weeks later I hauled out on a three-and-a-half-hour ride in the forest.

I think I was finally starting to understand how the concept, "Every time I fall I get back up again" was meant to go. What a dumb song. LOL

The Great Bobbinski

———

D EIRDRE PARTICIPATED in a half day cattle clinic in December while I was still stuck in my golf lesson stigma, so I just audited again. We didn't do as much arena riding during that winter because, honestly, it was too boring. But we still went up and saw the horses regularly and gave the arena our fifteen minutes of saddle time occasionally.

Around March, as we were rolling into our fifth year, we found Bobbi. She was a five-year-old fifteen-two hand, registered sorrel quarter horse. The broker we were working with, after we returned the other horse, had her available. Per his replacement guarantee, Deirdre reached out to him and set up an appointment to see her. Unfortunately, she had to work the day of the appointment, so I rousted up our best friends, yet one more time, to go with me and check out the horse.

From a looks standpoint, she was the most beautiful horse I had ever seen. The broker gave us a complete run down of his evaluation, and basically his only comment was that she was "a little forward in the lope." I had no clue what that meant, but it involved loping, so in and out it went.

I arrogantly prided myself on being more intelligent when looking at horses before I purchased them. I was no expert by any means, but I sure made it look good. My mother once told me, "If you can't dazzle them with brilliance, baffle them with bullshit." There ya go, I was giving it my best shot.

Our best friend and I both rode her around the arena. I asked the horse to do what little I knew, or so I thought anyway. The only concern I had was that her trot was a bit on the bouncy side. I had to keep in mind that, after Jesse and my compressed disc, I was spoiled with Montana's smooth trot. But I did not want the trot to necessarily be a game changer. We spent well over an hour riding and evaluating, asking questions, and receiving explanations and demonstrations. We struck a deal, loaded her up and headed home.

Once we got her home, we caught up with our trainer and asked if she would be willing to ride her and give us an evaluation. Deirdre and I watched from the wings as the trainer put Bobbi through the paces. We had no clue what we were watching but we saw Bobbi walk, trot, canter, bend, move her butt and move her shoulders. I am sure she had her do much more than what we noticed, but basically told us Bobbi was a keeper. However, she was going to require a lot of time and trail miles due to her age.

Deirdre wanted to take the lead on Bobbi's development, so for the next several months she alternated between Jesse and Bobbi when we hauled out. What little time we spent in the arena, she rode Bobbi almost exclusively.

Bobbi had been started in western pleasure and had an excellent foundation. She also has an excellent demeanor, but she lacked trail experience and miles. It only took a couple of rides for us to realize she was going to love being on the trail. It was a slow process to be sure, and every ride was a little adventurous. She soon started to learn there was an exciting life outside of an arena.

After finally convincing me that I would really enjoy myself, that spring Deirdre and I attended a half day "cattle clinic" together. I had virtually no idea what I was doing but Montana certainly seemed eager. Once she figured out what was going on, I just sort of held on and tried to go with the flow. As much as I hate to admit that I was being stubborn, I believe this cow sorting clinic was the catalyst that started to break down my 'golf lesson' phobia, but not quite yet.

Deirdre and I continued to ride the trails as much as possible. We took every opportunity to haul out and learn new trail systems with friends. After gaining more confidence, each of us would occasionally haul out alone to meet others to ride. We started to ride in large group events more often. It was all about riding trails.

How Far to the Gate

———

I T SEEMED LIKE WE WERE insanely obsessed with trail riding that summer. We were also becoming more cognizant about where we were riding in the forest. Many of the trails took us deep into the forest where cell service did not exist, and emergency access could be extremely difficult. I had always been the map reader and navigator, but it seemed maybe we should both know how to do those jobs. Deirdre learned how to read the GPS, read and follow a map, and keep track of where we were at any given point on a ride. Life would be made significantly easier with the advent of decent cell phone GPS tracking apps, but not for a while yet and definitely not until after this next story.

Mid-summer we decided, along with our best friend, to ride and explore a new system we had just discovered. A large state park offered a horse/snowmobile trail system to equestrians during the summer months. A new place and new trails. Sign us up. I easily found the trail system map online and set to work plotting a nice four-hour loop.

The weather on the day of the ride was absolutely perfect. Sunny skies, low humidity, very little wind and calling for a high temperature in the upper 70s. The horses were eager to ride and, for the most part, the trails were wide and easy. Well then again, they were snowmobile trails.

As you continue to read this memory, it may sound like I am just spewing a lot of mumble jumble at times. The truth is, that was how it felt as I tried to navigate the ride I planned for us that day.

Leaving the parking area, we picked up trail 18 at the trailhead of 14 and 18. According to the map, we would ride 18 until it terminated at the trailhead with trails 15 & 17 where we would pick up 15. The fun began when we discovered that trail 18 actually terminated on a dirt road that was the other end of trail 14. It took us a bit to figure out that we had to follow 14 for some distance toward 15 and 17. We followed 14 until it terminated on a black top road and there was no noticeable trailhead or trails anywhere in sight. Well now, that was interesting.

After exploring the area extensively, we pieced together that there really was not a defined trailhead "per say" as it seemed too appeared on the map. It was more like a "merge" point for six trails, each terminating at different places along a quarter mile strip of that blacktop road. Once we got that figured out, we determined that trail 15 must follow the blacktop road to the west for a while.

Revisiting the map, it looked like we would have to travel on the side of the road for about a mile before the trail re-entered the woods off the left side of the road. There were absolutely no markers along the blacktop road indicating that we were on 15 so we all kept a close eye out for the entrance to the trail off to the left. About an hour after we started down the road, we found trail 15 and were finally back in the woods.

Once into the woods on 15, we were an hour and a half into what I had calculated to be about a four-hour ride. That should have sounded an alarm in my head, but it didn't. I had used the map scale, and my computer screen, to calculate the distance of the ride. According to the map scale, we just rode about one mile in an hour. Our average riding speed is three miles per hour. If my head had done the math, I would have realized that section of road was at least three miles long, not one. We had been so focused on finding the trail, we never associated the time and distance. Rut-ro.

Most of the trails in the park were old dirt logging or access roads maintained by the park service for use by snowmobilers, horseback riders and hikers. As we rode down through a big ravine between two mountains, the ride was fairly easy and afforded us plenty of opportunity to relax, chat and lose track of time.

At about 13:00 trail 15 ended at a closed gate directly beside a cabin rental site. We could clearly hear children, dogs, and other activity on the far side of the cabin as we drew nearer. To avoid any potential issues, we called out to let the campers know we were there and on horseback.

Once we apparently got their attention, they all wandered out front to see the horses and riders. I have noticed that there is something about showing up unexpectedly on a horse that just seems to fascinate people. That was certainly one of those times.

It was at that trailhead that when we were supposed to be turning onto trail 16 that I first started to realize something wasn't quite right.

It took us about three hours to get there. The GPS was tracking us at an average "moving" speed of three miles per hour and indicated we had traveled eight miles. I knew all the GPS information was accurate. I had calculated the entire trip to be approximately thirteen miles, which should have been a four-hour ride, give or take. As I looked at the trail map and applied the GPS information to it, we were only about one-third of the way so far. Not a good feeling.

Wanting to confirm what I was rapidly starting to believe; I asked those great folks if they could show me on my map where exactly we were in the park. Then it got sort of funny. They had no clue how to read the map. I got it, I mean it was a trail map and it didn't really show any roads or such. Hell, I was struggling reading it.

To their credit they tried to help. "The road is over there," "there is another cabin circle across the road," and "the lake is up that way." But as far as telling me specifically where we were in the park, not so much.

After spending about ten minutes visiting and letting everyone pet the horses and feed them treats, we bid our farewells and headed for "the road over there."

It was pretty obvious on the map that trail 16 started somewhere off "the road over there", so we meandered over and found the cabin loop and then found trail 16. We found a safe place to stop and dismounted to take a break and stretch. I took the opportunity to show the girls the map, explaining that this was not where I thought we would be at this time of day. They understood what I was showing them but didn't seem too worried about it. Feeling a little better after I explained the situation, we mounted back up and proceeded down trail 16.

Then came the gnats.

Montana and I had been riding drag most of the ride with Deirdre and Jesse on point. It appeared that the first two riders got the bulk of the gnats and flies. I, on the other hand, didn't have much of an issue. Then again, I am a firm believer it is a better life through chemistry and am not sparing when it comes to spraying either my horse or myself.

After listening to the girls complaining and swatting their hands back and forth as we made our way down the trail, I finally volunteered to go on point and let the two of them ride behind me and get a little break. Now I had some flies and gnats, don't get me wrong, but I think I may have used a touch more bug spray because even on point they were not driving me down the crazy train road like they were the girls.

We had been riding for some time, and I wasn't really paying much attention to what they were doing behind me so, when I turned in my saddle to say something, I did a double take. The two of them had broken off long branches with leaves on them and were using them as swatters. They were waving them back and forth over the horse's necks as they just jaw jacked away. I chuckled to myself. Life is just awesome sometimes.

At 14:40 we arrived at the main gate at the south end of the park and Deirdre blurted out," I KNOW WHERE WE ARE."

She was all excited as she explained where we were located. At that point, I don't think the reality of our situation had occurred to her yet. I didn't have the heart to tell her just then, so I let her go on as we all dismounted and took another break and enjoyed our granola bars.

Just before we mounted back up to continue, I broke it to them.

The upside, Deirdre was correct on where we were. The downside, we were just barely over halfway through the ride. I also told them I thought it was shorter to continue than it was to return, but either way we still had a hike ahead of us. About half an hour after leaving the south gate we made a left onto trail 17. I think that was about the point when the girls realized we had been riding a very, very long time indeed.

For the first time they asked me where we were, how much further and about how long it was going to take to get to the trailers. I took time to show them on the map where I thought we were and where we needed to go. I explained that I could only guess at the time left based on what we had already ridden. I figured at the very soonest, we would be back to the trailers in about three more hours.

They seemed okay with everything I had just told them, so we rode on and to be honest, at that point, we were all getting a little punchy. We had been riding for almost six hours and we were all tired. Judging by the way we felt, we wouldn't make very good cowpokes or endurance riders I suspect.

Fortunately, the day was still absolutely stunning, and the gnats seemed to have settled down significantly. As we rode and continued to enjoy the day, they would occasionally ask where we were, and I would share my best calculation and show them on the map. The guy with the GPS knows all. I may not have been dead nuts on but, for the most part, I basically knew where we were.

The giggles started about 16:00. Suddenly, everything was funny.

Oh look, a bird, giggles.

Oh look, the horse sneezed, giggles.

Where is the gate, Rod? Just up a trail a bit, giggles.

At 16:45 a hiking trail intersected with our trail, and I told them I knew exactly where we were on the map, giggles. We were still at least well over an hour out, and we all giggled.

I have been married to Deirdre long enough to know the difference in her giggles. She's getting tired. And I have lived long enough to know that if one person starts giggling it soon becomes contagious. Next thing I knew, we were all giggling.

So, this is how the conversations went the last half hour on 17.

"Where's the gate, Rod?"

"Just around the bend," I replied.

Five minutes later: "How far to the gate?"

"Not far, just a bit more," I replied.

Five minutes later: "Are we almost to the gate?"

"Not much further, just over that knoll," I replied.

I was only guessing because up to this point, every time I thought I knew where we were without a physical reference, I was wrong. But I thought I would remain positive and let them think we were getting closer with each query they made. My sister would inform me on one of our future outings together that the correct response to such queries about 'where's the gate' is 'fourteen minutes.'

At 17:00 we finally reached the gate at the end of trail 17.

Trail 17 terminated on the blacktop road at that "merge" mess we had to figure out when we first started. Thank God we were there earlier because this time we didn't have to search; we knew exactly where to find 18 for the last leg to the trailers.

We were all giggly, tired, and relieved at the same time. We knew for certain how far we had to go to arrive at the trailers. We all needed a break off the horses, so we dismounted to walk around and stretch for a couple minutes. The trailers were only about half an hour away. My legs were tired and felt like they were going to cramp, so walking and stretching was a good thing, or so I thought.

When it was time to mount, I found a suitable step, put my left foot in the stirrup, lifted and swung my right leg back over the saddle when all of a sudden, YEOW. My thigh muscle was trying to pull my leg apart from my butt cheek to my knee. It hurt so badly it took all I had to not to cry like a little baby. Instead, I did what any true blooded male would do instead of crying: I cursed like a drunken sailor on a twenty-four-hour pass in Shanghai.

God, I love Montana. That horse just stood there as I clung to her for moral support, uttering every obscenity I had ever heard and even making up some new ones. It took about five minutes before the cramp subsided enough for me to even be able to walk a little to flex the muscle. The problem that still lay ahead of me was I had to remount and that was not something I was looking forward to asking my leg to do again.

My right leg was telling me: "Go ahead Rod, put that left foot in the stirrup and swing me over the cantle. I'll let you know how it goes." Yeah, I think I already knew how it was going to go.

Outsmart the leg, Rod. Yeah, that's the ticket.

Next to the gate was a rock that came up almost as high as Montana's belly. I figured it would make mounting easier, keeping leg swing to a minimum and less use of the thigh muscle. I brought Montana over to the rock and cautiously climbed up. The left stirrup was just a little below the rock, so I didn't put my foot in the stirrup, just leaned forward and ever so gently swung my leg back and over.

It worked. Just a little bit of tightness but I was able to sit and flex out the muscle and slip my foot in the stirrup. Life was good.

At 18:05 we finally arrived back at the trailers, eight-hours and thirty minutes after we left that morning. Twenty-two point three miles of trail was now behind us, as we took a few minutes to relax, stretch, and let the horses eat some hay before we loaded em up for the sixty-minute haul home.

As many times as I am reminded about that ride by my two companions, I have noticed that as bad as they say it was, it is also worn as a badge of honor, by all three of us.

Over the next two months that summer, we rode as much as we could, whenever we could. We wanted both horses and riders conditioned and ready to meet my sister at Iron Mountain in Virginia.

Over the Meadow.

———

I RON MOUNTAIN is located in the Jefferson National Forest. Riding the trails there is the same as riding trails in any National Forest. Unless there is a forest sanctioned trail system, nothing can be marked or flagged. If it is sanctioned, there are also plenty of outlaw trails that are not marked or mapped. If you ride out of a camp that is located within easy access to the forest, you are usually given a paper map and general directions and trail locations. Of course, for those of us who are wise and adventurous to the ways of trail riding, we were beyond confident we would find our way around hundreds of miles of unmarked trails just fine. And so, we did, for the most part.

The first day we traveled about ten miles along the VHHT to the Divide Trail and back, just to get a feel for the terrain. A long section of the VHHT was pretty much our base trail for all the rides out of camp. We would pick up the VHHT then follow it to the trailheads that connected to it.

The VHHT, Virginia Highlands Horse Trail, is located in the Mount Rogers National Recreation Area. The Virginia Highlands Horse Trail is a 68-mile trail between Elk Garden and VA Rt. 94. It features mountainous terrain, valley views and valley crossings. The trail includes parking and primitive camping for those who trailer horses. (6)

The second day we were fortunate enough to tie up with some riders in camp who knew the system, so they took us on a nice fifteen-mile ride over the northern section of trails. Most of the ride was spent on outlaw trails and, had we been alone, I am certain we would not have been able to find our way without getting lost. The trails followed dry creek beds, some worn trails, through thick scrub, old overgrown access roads to mention just a few of the conditions we encountered.

While working our way through a section of thick scrub and fallen limbs, we had the opportunity to once again enjoy another close-up meeting with our friends the ground bees. Running was out of the question due to the conditions and Deirdre and I were numbers six and seven in the line of eight riders. Thankfully the horses didn't go too crazy and the hive seemed small.

The best part of that ride was it took us past several reference points we would use for future rides. It gave us a much better handle on locations and landmarks that would help us navigate other trails & loops we would take over the next several days.

Some friends of my sister had also joined us for the first two days of our stay as they were working their way to another campground. They joined Deirdre and I as we celebrated our thirtieth wedding anniversary by reaffirming our vows on horseback at the camp. My sister officiated the ceremony and I got to kiss my beautiful lady while on our horses for the first time.

I know, getting a little mushy there Ca'boy, so move on.

As luck would have it, Hurricane Florence decided to work its way up the east coast during that trip. The forecast was sketchy but not horrendous, so we continued to plot our daily adventures. Every evening we made our way to the front porch of the office where the only internet was available. That front porch was also the only place where you could get an intermittent single bar of cellular service if you stood in just the right spot and didn't move. So, we would check the weather forecast and plan our daily ride accordingly. Eventually Florence would become a problem, but not for several more days.

On the third day we took a short seven-mile loop closer to camp and did some exploring. It was a momentous ride because my sister talked me into taking our one-year-old golden retriever Cisco to ride with us. During his first year, Cisco was not the most cooperative of puppies. Then one day it was like someone turned the stupid switch off and he became more in-tune. To my amazement, he did very well, never wandering far from the trail. From that day forward, he has ridden trail with us regularly and has steadily become "The Best Trail Dog Ever."

The fourth day we rode out the VHHT to the Divide Trail and climbed the half mile, six-hundred-foot ascent to the top for a nice eleven-mile loop around and back to camp. The Divide was a bit of a challenge as it had no switchbacks, a 26% grade on solid sheets of shale and required frequent stops to rest the horses.

"Lean forward and grab some mane." Ahh yes. Fondly recalled advice from our first long ride back home. Have you ever tried to get a good grip of mane on an Appaloosa? I leaned forward and held on to what I could.

Then came day number five and the Hugo Meadows ride.

The norm for trail maps on this trip were printed copies of someone else's GPS tracks or they were hand drawn. There was absolutely no usable scale on any of them. So, with map in hand, we headed out to ride what would end up an eleven-mile, five hour and forty-five-minute ride of fortitude, fear, and learning.

Our plan for that day was to follow the VHHT to Mikes Gap then pick up the trails (all from ride two) to "Frog Pond", then to "The Big Tree", then from there back to the VHHT and return to camp. On our way out the VHHT, we stopped to heed the call of nature at a reference point on the map called Hugo's Meadow.

The VHHT continued NE to Mike's Gap, well defined and easy to see, but there was also a less traveled trail that headed north from Hugo's Meadow as well. Our 'Not to Scale' map also showed the trail heading north from Hugo's Meadow that ended at the Frog Pond trailhead. Well, that was interesting, after all it was a "trail" that was clearly defined and on the map. The discussion soon turned to forest trail verses VHHT and ultimately to, "well maybe we can go that way instead."

I must admit, the trail out of Hugo's heading north looked well defined though perhaps a little less ridden. A ride on a forest trail is always preferable over a "bridle" trail as such, and after all it did end up at our destination trailhead.

Did I mention it was clearly explained to us when we were given our 'Not to Scale' trail map that it was old, and some of the trails on it may not exist anymore? If they did, they could be very hard to follow. Base camp was in a hollow at an elevation of 2500 feet. The mountains around us, and I do mean around us, all peaked between 3200 & 3600 feet.

When the discussion was over, we unanimously agreed the forest trail to the north was the way to travel. The three of us mounted our trusty steeds and headed up the trail. We slowly ascended the east side of the mountain on a well-defined trail. It was absolutely beautiful. We were so excited. Then we came to the Y.

Ahh yes, the Y. Located at the peak of the first mountain, elevation 2800 feet. It was decision time. Unsure which way to go, we decided to venture a short distance up both trails and check them out. The left seemed a bit more challenging than the right, so ultimately the right trail was chosen. We continued, ascending slightly up along the ridge and experienced some incredible views while sharing some great laughs.

Then we came to our first "major" ascent. It was far less aggressive than the day before so up we went like true horsemen. "There aint no mountain high enough." (7) After easily conquering that little obstacle, we continued a lazy ascent up to the peak along the narrow mountain ridge. The views over the descending sides of the trail surrounding us were incredible.

Then we came to another aggressive ascent. A little rockier, a little steeper. It was a little more challenging but absolutely within all our ability. After we nailed yet another obstacle, we once again continued our nice, gradual climb along the ridge.

In short order, we were on top of the world. We were standing in a 100- square foot area at an elevation of 3600 feet on the peak of the mountain. From where we stood, no matter which direction we looked, the mountain dropped off sharply and the surrounding view was breathtaking and spectacular. Talk about a photo op! There was simply no way to capture such amazing scenery on film and do it any justice at all. It was the pinnacle of our day. Oh hell, our entire trip.

After spending about 15 minutes or so reveling in the beauty, it was time to move on. We dropped down off the crown of the mountain and the first part of our descent started. A touch of seriousness began to fill the air as we started to pay closer attention to the trail. My sister was on point, Deirdre center, and I was drag. The conditions rapidly became more challenging as the angle of descent increased. The trail was covered with large, loose rocks and forward motion slowed to a crawl as we started to lean back and give the horses their heads. With each step, we began to pay closer and closer attention to what we were doing. Small talk was gone. Only pertinent information was being exchanged.

FROM MY SADDLE LIFE IS A GREAT ADVENTURE

"I have to stop; Jesse's saddle has slid forward." Deirdre's sudden loud, clear, concerned but not panicked voice cut through the sound of horse's hooves and the squeaking of saddle leather.

"There's a spot up a little further," my sister called back, spying a semi level place for her to dismount and correct her saddle.

"NO, I MEAN NOW," came the firm but definite response as I came to a stop behind her.

Her saddle had slid forward up and over Jesse's withers and was resting squarely on the horse's neck. Deirdre was already starting to dismount on the offside, which was uphill. In order to do so, she had to swing her left leg over the horse's head and slide down the right side of her neck. We had not yet learned the part about teaching your horse to tolerate every type of dismount you could imagine so thank goodness Jesse was cool.

Working on a steep and challenging slope, Deirdre quickly got her saddle squared away, offside mounted and we continued to slowly work our way down the mountain. I think deep down inside, we would have given our last drop of water for a switchback, but it was just not in the cards that day. The trail went straight down the side of the mountain brother.

It was not long until we hit the big slope. The trail descended on a 65% grade for about 150 feet and there was no way to avoid it and continue moving forward.

Analysis of the situation at this point: it was almost impossible to turn around and go back. Maybe with the knowledge we have today we would have tried, but it still would have been a very difficult challenge. At that point in our horsemanship journey, we hadn't learned "you are usually always safer on your horse," so dismounting and walking was the choice we all made. Today, we most certainly would choose to stay on the horses, but at that time continuing forward on foot was really our only option.

The slope was so steep, and having no traction from our cowboy boots, we found ourselves walking on the sides of our boots, holding on to saplings, trees, or branches so we would not slip and fall. Most of the rocks were about the size of footballs and loose. Every now and then one would break loose and tumble down the mountainside. I am still amazed they never hit one of us or one of the horses as they made their way down.

Single file, we inched our way down the 150 feet of steep trail. About a quarter of the way down Deirdre turned, looked up at me all serious like and quietly mouthed, "Oh Shit." How in the hell does she do that? Reading my mind. Unbelievable.

While I held on to a sapling with one hand and a rein in the other, Montana suddenly decided I wasn't going fast enough and nudged my shoulder with her nose.

"Montana you can't do that," I scolded her, as I took another step down on the side of my foot while reaching for another hand hold.

Apparently, Montana didn't get the message and she nudged me again. Down I went. Fear shot through me as all I could envision was rolling until I hit the bottom. Thankfully, a small tree stopped my fall and I quickly got up and grabbed the rein I lost.

After what seemed like light years we were safely at the bottom and checking to make sure we, the horses, and dogs, were all okay. Dogs? Never even thought about the dogs until we saw them sitting off to the side, eager to play some more. Then the nervous giggles came.

That obstacle was so far out of my skill set it wasn't funny, but we did it and we were all okay.

We descended from the mountain top more quickly than we had ascended. The remainder of the trail down from that point was steep but relatively easy. Soon we leveled out and it appeared that we were riding toward the Frog Pond trailhead once again. Yes, onward indeed. Until we hit the "T."

Based on what we thought the map was showing us, we should have come out at the Frog Pond trailhead. Instead, we hit a "T" onto another trail in the middle of nowhere. There was no "T" anywhere on the map other than trail heads we knew about, and this definitely was not Frog Pond. So, what trail did we just "T" with? Now that was the question of the day.

I heard that little voice in the back of my head: "Not to Scale map. Not all trails are still there or even on it. There are several outlaw trails that are not on it."

Decision: left, or right?

"Rod, where does the GPS tell us we are?"

"N36.48.48 / W81.03.23 – duh." I thought to myself because I didn't have the balls to say it out loud.

Overall evaluation: If we go right and the trail head is not there, we will end up by Raven's Cliff, a long way from home. We would have to turn around and back track to this point. If we go left, we will eventually end up on the VHHT again, but is there a mountain in between?

I looked at the map, I looked at the GPS track, I looked at the topo on the GPS, I took a compass reading and suggested that maybe we try left and see if we can get back to the VHHT.

About my GPS. The GPS was twenty plus years old then. (I still have that baby and use it every ride as a backup.) It can still accurately pinpoint my location within three feet of where I am at any time. It can show me the track that I follow once turning it on so I can back track if needed. It can show me topographical information about my surroundings. It can tell me how long I have been moving and at what speed and direction along with an endless list of other information. Unfortunately, it cannot show me trails or trailheads in relationship to current position. I can plug in trailhead coordinates and make them a waypoint, but I wasn't able to now because the only map is "Not to Scale" and lacks a longitude and latitude grid.

The trail to the left was easy to see and headed in the *"GENERAL"* direction back to the VHHT. I can read a compass. I knew the VHHT was SW of our current location, based on the recent track shown on the GPS. The topo of the area where we were currently located indicated we would have to ascend to get back to the VHHT. If we followed a fairly direct path, it would be a steady grade working up the side of the mountain. What I could not tell was where exactly we were on our Not to Scale map or if the trail was going to turn and climb the mountain again.

I explained all of this and, based on everything I said, we decided to try going left. About a quarter of a mile up the trail another discussion developed between the three of us.

The girls: "We are continuing to climb."

Me: "Yes, we are. I told you we most likely would."

The girls: "We're not comfortable going back up the mountain we just came down."

Me: "Okay, I get that. All I can tell you is this trail is going in the general direction to intersect the VHHT, paralleling our path earlier. No matter what, we will have to ascend to get there."

The girls: "We think we need to go the other way."

Me: "I am not sure about that. Are you willing to back track just in case it's the wrong choice?"

The girls: "Yes."

I have learned that if someone believes firmly about a direction, then we should try it. I am not ashamed to admit I have been wrong more than once. We turned the horses around and headed out the other way. Personally, I would have continued. However, I had absolutely no solid reasoning I could give them to do so, other than that is what I felt to be correct. We were all together, so I was good with the decision to turn around.

As it turned out, we did eventually hit the Frog Pond trailhead and from that point finding the campground was easy. Later that evening when I downloaded the GPS track into the computer, I saw that if we had not turned around and found Frog Pond, we would have slowly worked our way up the side of the mountain and ended up back at Hugo's Meadow and the VHHT. At that "Y" I suspected. A win, win I believe, it would have been either way.

On the sixth day, the trails were shut down in the forest due to Hurricane Florence. The rain was pretty steady with some swelling streams and really wet conditions. Our sites were in the lowest part of the campground next to a stream that was known to overflow and flood the sites, so we decided to cut our trip short by two days and head home. Although we left early, we still made some really great memories.

During the haul home, Deirdre and I started to seriously talk about taking some lessons or attending some clinics to learn more about riding. There have been several times now in the last few years that we were lucky to get through some difficult situations. Looking back, I have to give credit where it is due, and that is to the horses. Quite

111

honestly, most of the time we just asked them to go and let them figure it out as we held on. Yeah, maybe it was time.

Based on all the excitement with Jesse's saddle sliding up her neck, we also discussed introducing cruppers into our tack line up. Once again Deirdre did "our" due diligence researching and asking other riders for insight on how to use them. By December we were ready to start the introduction process with the horses.

Tail of the Crupper

_____

W E STARTED OUT WORKING on the ground, slowly introducing the crupper to the girls. First, we tacked up and led them around the arena. Obviously, we figured they needed to get used to something new being jammed up under their tail and preferred they get used to it without us in the saddle. A little bit more knowledge about the teaching process might have helped avoid the outcome.

For the most part, all three horses seemed to handle it okay on the ground. We gave them about two hours of ground time spread out over multiple days to come to terms with a piece of leather tucked up under their tail and pushing against their butts before we decided to get on.

Since Bobbi's arrival seven months earlier, Deirdre had been her primary rider alternating between her and Jesse. It was simply luck of the draw that Bobbi was chosen that morning instead of Jesse. She tacked her up with the crupper and I tacked up Montana. We planned just a short ten to fifteen-minute ride, slow and easy, to make sure they were handling the new piece of tack okay.

We had ridden about ten minutes and Montana, and I were doing fine. Deirdre and I met up mid arena and she told me she was concerned because Bobbi felt tense and a little excitable. We decided it would be best to just end the ride at that point and come back the next day and work on it again.

Then I uttered those famous last words, "Okay. Let's just ride over to the front wing doors and dismount."

As we started to traverse the short fifty feet to the gate Bobbi exploded. I felt helpless as I watched her bucking and throwing her back legs while Deirdre hung on for dear life. She looked like she was riding the prize bronc in the rodeo. I swear Bobbi could have kicked the ceiling lights out if they were any lower as she bucked and twisted. We knew nothing about trying to disengage the hips. We had learned nothing about maintaining a proper seat or how to attempt an emergency dismount. There was no night latch to grab. I watched in horror as Deirdre held on for about four seconds before Bobbi literally launched her through the air.

It felt like an eternity before I was able to dismount and reach her lying there on the floor of the arena. My heart was racing in my chest as I raced over to her lying there motionless on the ground. I bent down to help her up, only to hear her scream when I touched her. There are a number of things we experience in life that really, really suck, and that situation squarely rated as one of my top two.

Five nondisplaced pelvic fractures and a complete separation of the top of the humerus from her right shoulder. She was stabilized at our local hospital and transported to a larger hospital and underwent surgery for the shoulder, which required installing a plate and screws. Then she had to begin rehab for both pelvis and shoulder. She spent just over a week in the hospital and two more weeks in a rehab facility before she finally was able to come home with a wheelchair and walker. Several more weeks of physical therapy, as well, just to walk.

While she was recovering, and doing her PT, I had the opportunity to re-evaluate the whole situation and what happened. In short, as I am learning more and more, it was rider knowledge or lack thereof that contributed to what happened that morning. With the help of our trainer, we determined the crupper was the issue. Bobbi was trying to tell us that all along, we just didn't answer the phone soon enough. There were several things we should have done differently, had we been more knowledgeable, such as more ground time and different exercises. We should have recognized the horse's personality change and asked ourselves why. A different style or smaller crupper, perhaps. Ultimately, we were not experienced enough to understand what the horse was telling us or how to properly introduce a new piece of tack. We eliminated the crupper and have not had a problem with her since.

After that incident, I finally gave up the golf game B.S. and decided to participate in a real clinic and start to learn how to ride properly. But first, I needed to step over Deirdre's accident. I decided I needed to ride Bobbi. If you have ever been involved in an incident where someone was seriously hurt on a horse, then you know there is a part of you that is nervous about getting up on that horse for the first time afterwards. That winter, I enrolled Bobbi in a training program. Although her personality remained awesome after the crupper was eliminated, she was still only five years old. Having a professional work with her, and then work with me, had way more positives than negatives.

By spring, as the riding season got underway, I began to ride Bobbi almost exclusively. In April after completing her therapy, Deirdre was finally able to mount up again. Once we started back on the trails, she alternated between Montana and Jesse. Although I rode all three of our horses, it would mainly be me and "The Great Bobbinski" from that point on.

He's Gonna Hit the Wall

I SIGNED UP FOR two clinics that spring. A one day "Cowboy Only" clinic and a five day "Advancing Your Horsemanship" clinic being held at our facility. The Cowboy Only clinic was a bunch of guys and the clinician who taught us about groundwork in the morning and riding in the afternoon. Sort of like testing the waters with my toe type of thing.

With the one day "Cowboy Only" under my belt, I was excited and ready to start the five-day Advancing Your Horsemanship clinic. How fortunate for me that it started the day after the clinic I had just attended.

The first day went quite well. During the morning, the clinician covered some of the same groundwork we had learned and worked on the day before, plus some new exercises. That afternoon we rode several simple patterns, mostly at a walk, or a trot if we were comfortable. Thinking back, I believe the clinician used that first day to evaluate each of the riders and determine their skill level. As for me? I thought it was a great day. I walked and sometimes trotted easily around the patterns as we performed the exercises. Yes indeed, by the end of day one, I concluded I was going to like this clinic stuff.

At the daily briefing the next morning, the clinician outlined the plans for the coming day. As I listened intently, I didn't think the plan for the day sounded too scary, so I was pumped to get started. I should probably have paid a little more attention to the part where he mentioned he was going to push each of us just a little outside of our comfort zone.

We started the morning with some quick basic groundwork or lunging of the horses to "get the stink off." Then we mounted our horses and did a couple of laps around the arena in a walk and then a trot, back to a walk then turned and went the other direction. As we rode around the arena, he talked to the group or sometimes an individual, pointing out or explaining what we should be doing.

My first big change came when he stopped me and said, "Rod, I am going to raise your stirrups up."

Okay. I stopped and waited as he raised my stirrups up so far it felt like my knees were going to hit my Adams apple. In reality, he only raised them a couple of inches, but after five and a half years it felt like a mile. He explained to me why he was doing it and how it was going to help improve my riding. Even though I was a bit uncomfortable at first, the new position started to grow on me pretty quickly.

By the end of day two, I felt like my brain was going to explode.

I heard: Opening and closing doors. Lead out with the inside hand, down and off neck with the outside hand. Lean back further than you ever have in your life then lean back more. Look where you want that horse to go and don't pull on its face. Sit straight and don't lean into that turn. Stop straight and take two steps back. Don't pull on that horse's head but don't have too loose a rein. The list goes on and on and on. And we trotted a lot that day. I mean, A LOT.

Day three was an extension of day two on steroids.

Things were moving faster in the saddle now and the input of information was overwhelming. Just about every exercise we did required us to trot, or a canter for the more advanced riders. My right hand had a blister from holding the night latch so much that I had to start wearing my leather riding gloves. My body was exhausted from all the trotting. My head was spinning from all the information. When we broke for lunch, I just sat in the corner of the clubroom like a vegetable as I ate, thinking "What the hell did I get myself into." But after lunch I got back out there.

At the end of day three I was in information overload.

I heard so many things I had never heard before and knew I was never going to remember it all. At the end of each day, I tried diligently to jot down notes to help remind me later of all the things I had learned or heard. At the end of the third day, I struggled to write down anything because I could not stay focused on one thought long enough before something else pushed it aside. I felt shot and ready to throw in the towel.

I dragged myself out of bed at five 'o'clock that fourth morning and, with my brain blurred with half-baked thoughts, made my way to the clinic for yet one more day of mental overload and physical torture. To my overwhelming joy and excitement, I learned at the morning briefing we were moving into "Advanced Horsemanship." Not to worry, Rod, it was not going to be anything big or difficult, just how to set up and execute proper lead departures and flying lead changes.

Thank God the clinician knew that was well above my skill set. He never asked me to go faster than a trot. The other riders in the clinic were awesome, explaining what I was watching as people would perform the exercises. I listened and watched intently, trying to see and understand what they were telling me was happening. To be honest, I wasn't always sure what they were saying or what I was seeing.

At lunch I didn't even eat, opting instead to lean back in a chair over in the corner and close my eyes. I was done. I hit the wall so hard I thought all my teeth were going to fall out. There was not one part of me that found any of this enjoyable anymore. I wanted to quit so badly but I couldn't, I just couldn't. Whether it was being taught never to quit or just plain stupidity, I would force my way through the entire five days then determine what the future held for me as far as clinics were concerned.

At the end of day four there was not much more than a shell of me as I headed to my truck to go home and collapse. Our trainer, who had convinced me I would benefit from this five-day clinic, intercepted me before I reached the truck.

"How ya doing Rod?"

"This is way over my head," I sighed, with what had to sound like total defeat in my voice.

"This is a lot of information in a very short amount of time, and I know it seems overwhelming, but what you are learning here will benefit you more than you realize." She is not one for long drawn-out comments. She gets to the point, and to this day, I have yet to see any of the points she has made not be on the mark.

"See you in the morning?" She asked, or was it encouragement? I suspect she could clearly see the defeat in my body language.

"I'll be here," I replied with all the enthusiasm I could muster. Believe me, it wasn't much.

I really wanted to quit at the end of that fourth day. Just wanted to hang up my spurs, well maybe my boots because I didn't use spurs yet, tuck my tail between my legs and run home to mama.

I had been seriously considering not showing up for day five. It was that short brief conversation with my trainer that motivated me just enough to get up the next morning and drag my sorry ass to the clinic.

I arrived on day five exhausted, overwhelmed, brain dead, and sore. But I was there. Six days of clinic. Six hours each day in the saddle. What was I thinking when I decided to do that? BUT I WAS THERE. And today we were going to chase cows.

I was beyond thrilled, NOT even a little bit.

After our morning briefing in the clubroom, I leisurely tacked up Bobbi and headed out to tackle yet one more day of fun and excitement. As Bobbi and I rode around the arena checking out the penned cows, my mind wandered back to the first camping and riding trip with my sister. I remembered the clinician there talking about sorting during one of the events. I recalled her saying, "If your horse has never worked a cow, they are going to love it. Horses love cows."

I was not quite sure if I was buying that theory quite yet, since my six-year-old mare was trying to figure out what those large, possibly horse eating things were. With my hand yet again securely in my night latch, we passed back and forth by the cows several times until they became just another part of the arena to her.

I started that morning exhausted and feeling like my brain could not process one more nugget of wisdom about horses. I could not for the life of me see any purpose to working cows. I had done a cow sorting clinic previously and could not justify putting my exhausted body through it again that day. As I was tacking up to start the day, I decided since I was here, I would ride until lunch, call it a wrap on learning and go home, grab a glass of scotch, and pass out on the couch. I mean, what the hell was I going to learn pushing around cows?

In the morning session, the clinician had us working as a group as he explained and taught us the basics of moving cows. Herding them, staying in the eye, turning them, leading them, communicating with the other riders, and working as a team. That morning went unbelievably fast. As I entered the clubroom for lunch that day, I had already scrapped my earlier plan to leave. I wolfed down my lunch and found myself ready to get back out there with those cows. I was going to stay the course and I didn't even realize I was excited.

What happened that afternoon would change my outlook on horsemanship forever.

That afternoon we separated into two-man teams for individual cow work. We sorted, we drove, we contained, and we worked them in ways I never knew possible. I was nervous and braced as I started doing the exercises, but the clinician was always right there watching and directing me on what to do.

The most common correction I heard during the past six days was, "ROD, LEAN BACK AND TIGHTEN YOUR CORE." I could not even guess the number of times I heard that. Every time I heard it, I did what I thought I was supposed to do. By the afternoon of that sixth day, I had heard it one time too many and realized I obviously was not getting it.

So, when he yelled it that last time.

"ENOUGH," I yelled back at him, and I stopped my horse. "I have tried to sit back and tighten my core every time you remind me. Come and explain to me exactly what you want me to do." I think maybe some of my weeklong frustration was reflected in my tone. Just saying. To his credit, he just took it in stride.

He walked over and I explained to him what I was trying to do every time he told me to "lean back and tighten my core." He then helped physically adjust me in my seat to sit back and showed me what he meant by tightening my core.

Well, I'll be. So that is what the beginning of a proper seat is supposed to feel like! It would take some time to retrain my muscles, and replacing my current saddle with one that was designed to help me sit properly, but I would get there eventually.

That afternoon just got better and better. Bobbi and I went back out there and chased those cows with a whole new enthusiasm. As things started to pick up speed, I was concentrating way more on the cow than on what I was doing. We were making quick stops, turns and fast departures. We were stepping into canters and back to trots. I was moving cows, and I was riding my horse, having a blast. To be completely honest, it was Bobbi who made it happen most of the time, I just sort of thought about what I should be doing. Bobbi and I were a team focused on working together on a job. It was AWESOME.

As exhausted as I was going into that day, by the time we were done, I was pumped. I not only realized how much I had learned over those six days but was able to put it to practical use as well. During that last afternoon, I recalled so much of what I thought I would never remember. Don't get me wrong, in the scheme of things, we were still a novice team and pretty much sucked. I am sure that was quite clear to everyone present. But, to Bobbi and me, We Were Champions.

A couple of weeks later I ran into our trainer, and she asked if I had enjoyed the clinic and if I would consider participating in another one. I explained that it was a serious sensory overload and was sure I would only retain about ten percent of the information overall. I also told her had it not been for the cattle on the last day, I don't think I would readily jump right into another clinic. But I also told her it taught me the importance of learning to become a better rider, not just for myself but for my horse.

The truth is, when I was riding properly, I could feel my horse becoming an extension of me. When we are both on the same page, my fear became awareness, and my understanding became trust. I was starting to realize that as I became a better horseman, she would be a better horse. To me that equated to a safer and more enjoyable ride all around.

My answer to "would you do another clinic? was a resounding yes! However, I told her I needed to give myself some time to work on what I had just learned and become a bit more proficient at the very basics. But I would absolutely sign up for more clinics as well as continue to seek knowledge and help.

"Wait a second. Life is great. We're Champions"

"We're Good!! I don't know why I get so down on us"

"Now we're getting the hang of this"

"It's working"

"I'm Excited"

"I was wrong. We suck"

"Ugh,This is hard"

"I messed up"

"I think I should go back to cleaning stables"

A day in the life of an Equestian

Later that day while I was preparing dinner at home, I heard a 'ding' telling me I had received a message on my phone. My trainer had sent me this graph. It would be the first solid building block that would define our future relationship.

(8)

Practical Use

A FTER THE CLINIC, I started thinking more about how I did things on my horse every time I rode. How I asked her to move. How aggressive or soft I was. Was I using a cue instead of just kicking or pulling. I knew I had a long, long way go before I would be doing things correctly but for the first time, I was starting to ask the questions. I noticed the responses I received to my questions and was beginning to see a different relationship developing with my horse.

I rode all that summer trying to apply what I had learned on the trails. When I was stumped or confused, I sought out advice. I also started using the arena to practice and did not find it quite as boring. Overall, it was a very active summer full of learning and advancement. Who would have thought hard work was going to be so much fun?

Our big summer outing that year was to East Fork TN to meet up with my sister for a week of riding. To our extreme pleasure the rides were all tame with no crazy adventures to share. We rode sixty-five miles of trails through gorgeous forests to some of the most beautiful overlooks and vistas we had seen so far.

Deirdre took another three-day clinic in the fall, and I saddled up for another "Cowboy Only" clinic.

I love the "Cowboy Only" clinic. Not just because it's just a bunch of guys riding horses, my trainer helps the clinician so there you have it, but because it makes learning fun. Seriously, when you get a bunch of guys on horses together just to have fun while learning, it's a blast. I cannot tell you what it is exactly that makes the "Cowboy Only" clinic so much fun. Maybe it's like a guy's day out or something, I don't know.

FROM MY SADDLE LIFE IS A GREAT ADVENTURE

Anyway, all I know is that we laugh, try hard, bust balls, motivate each other, and go away better horseman than when we started.

During the clinics I attended, I noticed that the rider's skill level varies from complete novice to folks that could probably be clinicians themselves. There are people that have ridden since childhood without ever taking a lesson to folks that just want to learn something new. What I like most about the clinician I ride with most often is that he evaluates the riders individually during the first few hours. Then, as the clinic progresses, he works with each rider based on their skill level and develops their trust through comfort. Without realizing it, he maneuvers us outside our comfort zone just enough to see changes and make a difference.

When I started the five-day clinic, I could walk easily through the exercises. I could trot okay. I was scared to death of cantering. When the clinic started, he let me walk all the exercises and I was at ease. He praised my use of proper leg cues, rein management and riding ahead of my horse. He let me walk until he knew I was not nervous during an exercise, then he asked me to try at a trot. Just try. He explained what I had to do; how I had to sit, where I had to put my hands and legs. Then he had me start walking and verbally guided me into the trot, telling me how to correct my equitation as we rode. Sometimes he rode right beside me, sometimes he would just watch from his horse. BUT the way he did it made me believe in myself, which gave me the confidence to do it.

The point is his teaching method made me want to take more clinics. I gained more knowledge and for the first time the indoor arena was starting to become a useful tool.

As the year drew to a close, Deirdre and I had covered about five hundred trail miles.

125

During the winter, I sent Bobbi back to her trainer for three months. I had ridden her almost exclusively the entire year, but she was still young and needed more work than I was qualified to handle. That winter she was taught how to drive from the hindquarters rather than reaching with the front, to eliminate the "forward in the lope." While Bobbi spent the winter with her trainer, Montana and I spent the winter practicing what we had learned over the summer in the clinics. I was still far from proficient, but I had kept good notes to which I could refer.

I'm not sure what happened over the summer that triggered me to want to learn. I was realistic enough to know I was not ready for flying lead changes or anything like that, but I knew I needed to concentrate more on groundwork and basics in the saddle. I suddenly had this craving to become better. To build a better house I needed to build a more solid foundation.

That winter I spent just about every morning in the arena. Two days a week with Deirdre, and four days by myself. I did not want to lose my connection with Bobbi while she was in training, so I split up my groundwork days between her and either Montana or Jesse. Some days I would have two or even all three of them in the arena with me. The days I worked on riding it was usually with Montana, so Bobbi was fresh for her daily training. I was practicing everything I had learned in the clinics and taking lessons on Bobbi from her trainer.

I certainly had my fair share of single digit temperatures to ride in those winter months. I cannot lie, it was a real struggle getting dressed and finding the motivation to head to that un-heated barn when it was only six degrees outside. But there was something driving me. As much as I would have happily stayed home on those frigid days, once I was at the barn and working with my horse, the temperature just didn't seem to matter.

There truly is "Something about the outside of a horse that is good for the inside of a man." (9)

By spring I had developed a much better seat, still not good, but better. I was still not great at my leg cues but was getting better. My rein management still sucked but had improved as well. I tossed out the lightweight reins I tied in a knot and replaced them with nice, weighted, split reins. I was now leading out with each hand rather than pulling/pushing on the horse's face. My comfort level with trotting and posting had greatly improved but I was still way short of a controlled canter. I would continue to work on both.

With the arrival of June, Deirdre and I already had about two-hundred trail miles under saddle for the season. During that month I attended a three-day clinic with Deirdre and another of my favorite 'Cowboy Only" clinics. Our knowledge was growing, not just in the saddle but about the saddle and how it fit. We broke down and invested in saddles that not only fit our horses better but also improved our seat and equitation tremendously.

If we weren't on the trails, we were in the arena practicing what we had learned. When we found ourselves struggling, we would seek advice. As much as the clinics and learning were assisting us in the arena, they were also affecting our trail riding abilities. We found ourselves constantly discussing and using what we learned to help maneuver the horses better out on the trail.

Deirdre and I would each do a couple more clinics, once in August and then again in October. We were moving along and starting to understand there was more to riding than kick to go, pull to stop and yank to turn.

Hang On Beanie Boy

———

A T THE CLINIC in October, we were in the outside arena working on a nine-cone pattern at the trot and canter. The clinician apparently thought it was time for me to push the outside of the envelope and pick it up a notch and try to canter. He kept it simple at first by asking me to trot the four small square patterns that made up the large nine-cone pattern. When I finished my four little squares at a trot, he wanted me to pick up a canter and ride around the outside of the entire nine-cone pattern and stop back at the other riders.

I completed the four small squares and then went about setting Bobbi up for a departure. I had set her up a couple of times (sort of) during the clinic, but my departures were rough, and the canters were short and horrible. I tried to remember everything I heard when he had explained it earlier. Left lead, easy now Rod, ask for a slight inside eye, inside leg slightly forward start the bend and then bring the outside leg back and ASK for the canter.

And a canter I got. Bobbi stepped up into a lope and we were truckin. I had no idea at all what to was about to happen once we started. As we continued our trip around those nine-cones, all that kept going through my mind was "Stop the merry-go-round I want to get off." To Bobbi's credit, she continued to canter around and around and around that pattern.

I felt like I was rocketing around the arena at speeds that would have put a racehorse to shame. I could hear the clinician yelling, "The more you squeeze and the harder you pull, the worse it is going to get."

Seriously? "The more you squeeze and the harder you pull the worse it is going to get" was the advice I received? How was that going to

128

stop this four-legged, eleven-hundred-pound land speed record setting animal from killing me?

All kidding aside, my brain and body were in total survival mode. It didn't matter what I heard or what I was told, I was hanging on with every part of my body I could hold with while my arms flailed for some kind of balance. Everything I had learned went out the window and I was back to pulling her face to stop. I have no idea how many times I circled those cones, but it sure felt like a whole lot.

Suddenly there was a horse running alongside Bobbi and me. The owner of our stable, Bobbi's winter trainer, thank God, was there to save me. As the two of us raced around that arena I could hear her speaking. She was most likely yelling but I only heard a muffled voice. At first, I didn't comprehend a single word she was saying, then I slowly began to realize she was giving me instructions as she rode no more than a couple feet from my left side.

Then I started to hear the words. BREATH, LEAN BACK, PUT YOUR HANDS FORWARD, RELAX YOUR LEGS. Seriously? I'm on a horse traveling at the speed of light and you want me to relax? She stayed right there with me, at my side, and kept repeating it over and over again. I slowly started to believe she was trying to help me. Obviously, I needed to change something, or this nightmare was never going to end.

I think I started with the leaning back part. I had been told to lean back so many times in clinics that I knew it would change the way I sat the horse. Slowly at first, until I felt myself moving my hips with the flow instead of bouncing.

"Good, good," she hollered after I sort of settled into a half assed rhythm. "Hands forward."

Feeling just a little bit more balanced, I reached forward ever so slightly. I immediately felt a change in the horse, and she seemed to come down just a little.

"Now try and relax your legs and take them off her." That was the point where I was about to put all my trust and what I perceived to be my life, into the hands of another person and a wild horse.

Slowly, while leaning back with my hands forward, I eased my legs off the horse.

Suddenly my entire world was no longer a blur as it flew by me. Bobbi slowly transitioned down to a walk. Holly crap-a-rollie I survived.

I cannot tell you how profoundly that entire event affected my attitude toward learning and working to become a better rider. The fact that I was running out of control, and another rider was able to ride with me and talk me down to a walk, left an impression on me that I will never forget.

This took place on the last half of the last day of that clinic. I am certain the clinician purposely did not ask me to canter again that day, and I was sure not complaining about it. However, after that I swore to myself I would learn how to ask for, get and be able to ride a controlled canter. A task I have gotten much better at but am still working diligently at to this day.

We participated in more clinics in our seventh year than we would over the next couple of years as events around the world started to change how we lived as a society. The desire was there but availability and cost would cause a slowdown in that particular area. To compensate, we started taking occasional lessons from our trainer to help us work on any details we struggled with. The insight and help she gave us was invaluable. As much as the clinics helped me reach outside my comfort zone and provide knowledge, working with her gave me detailed explanation and guidance. Even an hour with her helped determine the specifics as to what I needed to work on because it was focused specifically on my needs.

We finished the year with a little over six hundred trail miles as we rolled into winter and our arena work began in earnest once again.

Epiphany

─────

O NCE AGAIN, DEIRDRE AND I SPENT every day she was
off in the arena together and I was generally there the days she
worked, as well. Between the clinics and the lessons, we came up with
so many things we could put together and work on in the arena that we
easily lost track of time. Amazing. To think that only a couple years ago
we were ready to shoot ourselves from boredom after fifteen minutes in
the arena. Now we had to remind ourselves to stop after a couple of
hours and not ride it till it broke.

That winter we got pretty creative during our arena workouts. We made
obstacles that imitated cutting branches, hauling limbs, moving fallen
objects with ropes as if dragging branches. We worked on opening
and closing gates, moving things on the ground with sticks instead of
dismounting. We used culvert pipes to step over, tarps to step on and
bridges to walk over. Anything we encountered on the trail we tried to
reproduce. We set up cone patterns in all shapes and sizes. We practiced
at a walk, trot, and canter. We were anything but bored in the arena that
winter.

We attended two clinics that year, along with taking several lessons, and
rode the trails. Lots and lots of trails. The clinics and lessons taught
us so many things that were useful on the trail, but my favorite was
probably learning to counter bend and how to control the shoulders.

"What does controlling the shoulders have to do with trail riding?
Well, just about everything." The words of the day. I still remember that
clinic when I learned how to counter bend. It was kind of like learning
to canter around the cones only this time I just plain did not get it.

The exercise was to walk the horse up the rail at about a forty-five-degree angle while asking for the inside eye and moving the shoulder, placing the horse in a slight "C" bend. I could walk her up the rail at a forty-five in a side pass, I could even ask for the inside eye, but I just could not get the bend. The clinician explained it to me again and again, but I just didn't get it.

We did the exercise just before lunch then moved on to something else before we took a break to eat. As everyone headed out to eat lunch, Bobbi and I stayed out in the arena and tried to figure out how to do it. I tried more eye and still got a basic side pass. I tried less eye and got a basic side pass. I tried more barrel pressure and got out of the proper angle. I tried more shoulder pressure and she turned away from the wall.

Forty minutes into lunch I was still out there trying to figure it out when the clinician came into the arena.

"Rod, first of all, you think you need to steer this horse with the reins like you are driving a car," he starts out. "I want you to put the reins down on the neck of the horse and put both hands on the pommel. Now, using just your legs, I want you to turn the horse to the left.

"Good. Now stop her and turn her to the right. Good. The horse does not need the reins to steer. You just moved that horse using her shoulders. That is the key." He then proceeded to walk me through the entire process. One detailed step at a time he taught me how to get a counter bend. It was like an epiphany! Once I understood it, I got it, and it was incredibly easy.

I have learned many things over the years, but learning how to control the shoulders rates up there in the top three when it comes to usefulness on the trail.

Enter the GPS App

———

IN LATE SPRING WE SET OUT on a trail ride to find a local waterfall in the forest. We had never ridden in that area before, but we had a friend who rode there several years before and was willing to try to remember how to get there from the trailhead. As we headed out that morning in late May, we were excited about riding somewhere new.

The evening before, I had familiarized myself with the topo of the area so I would have an idea of what to expect from the terrain. I also assumed that there were going to be some sort of trails to take us to and from the waterfall. When we left the trailhead that morning, the topography was as I expected but the trails were a little more than a bit shy of passable. It was not surprising when we quickly found ourselves in a "ride and find" situation.

It did not take long to realize that the trails as they were remembered were no longer passable. Not an uncommon situation for trail riders. Unless trails are ridden regularly and at least partially maintained overgrowth, tree falls, and washouts soon make them difficult to see or use.

I'm not much for thanking the government for anything, but I am thankful for GPS. I also like smart phones for giving us the ability to see our location in real time on a satellite image anywhere on the planet. When I ride new areas, I still like physical maps, when I can get my hands on them, and I always use two professional handheld GPS units for additional tracking.

So, I began using smart phone GPS tracking apps that summer. Like most guys I like cool, new toys and those Apps really fit the bill.

We started out a little shaky and had to bushwhack our way to an oil lease road we could see on the App. The bushwhacking was a little interesting at times, and getting out of the woods and up on the road was a bit of a challenge, but we got-er done without incident. Once we were on the road it was just a matter of following forest and oil lease roads to the falls and then returning.

Once we made it to the falls, we tied off the horses and took a break for pictures and a bite to eat. While we were chilling, I took the opportunity to scope out the tracking app a little closer. It looked like we could easily cut off a huge portion of road by taking a route around the top of the mountain, then skirt the edge of two fairly large fields, a clear-cut section, and pick up what looked like an old logging road. If I was correct, we would end up just above the parking area on the trail we started from. I showed this to the other three, explained what I saw and thought, and we all agreed to give it a shot.

I know from experience that the satellite view being used will most likely be several years old. What you see on the app does not necessarily mean that is what you will see when you get there.

The first large field was almost exactly like the satellite view. The second large field was considerably more overgrown, but we were able to track through it okay. The clear-cut however was nothing like the view. If it had not been for the gas line that ran directly through it in exactly the direction we thought we should take, we would have had to turn back.

Once we started across the clear-cut, we saw that the gas line would terminate on an oil lease road which we could clearly see on the app. That road circled back to the main road we originally took on our way to the falls. An old logging road I could see on the app should have been on the right about a hundred feet before we hit the oil lease road. But the clear-cut was much too overgrown, and we could not find it.

Here was the thing. When we reached the oil lease road, we were about one tenth of a mile above the trail we had ridden before we started bushwhacking. It was only five hundred feet away and just over two hundred feet below us. Rechecking the satellite view again and evaluating the density of the surrounding forest, I figured we could bushwhack through the woods for about a hundred feet to the beginning of the descent, then work long switch backs down the side of the mountain to the trail.

Once again, I explained my thoughts and we all agreed to give it a try, so we headed into the forest. When we reached the descent, it was obvious that bushwhacking switchbacks was not going to happen. Rather than just give up entirely, we decided to walk east along the edge and look for a clear place to descend. The woods got a touch dicey and dense at times, but we did find a fairly clear way down that was almost dead nuts on top of the trail below.

While looking for a place to descend, we had slowly dropped down about one-hundred feet in elevation which left only about a one-hundred-foot descent over a distance of two-hundred feet. Shades of Hugo's Meadow entered my mind as I evaluated what lay ahead.

There were some fallen trees we needed to step over. There was thick brush we would have to work through, and we would definitely need to watch our footing carefully.

Hugo's Meadow versus that descent. Knowledge, better fitting tack, better seat, better control of the horse and the immortal words of our trainer, "You are always safer on your horse."

Deirdre and I were definitely in and the rider who was familiar with the area was in. Our best friend looked at that descent and simply said, "OH HELL NO."

After some discussion we decided that the three of us were going to ride and she was going to walk. Either way was fine, we would all still be together. Down we went. Lean back, hands forward, legs off. Watching, looking, stepping, slowing, and stopping until we reached the bottom safe and sound on the trail that we wanted.

When our friend joined us all she said was, "You guys are all nuts." We all busted out laughing.

In addition to clinics that summer, Deirdre and I participated in a local Extreme Cowboy Association (EXCA.) (10) event. The event challenged us to ride a pre-arranged pattern through a detailed obstacle course in the arena while being judged. There were various riding categories that dictated the degree of challenge depending on rider age, experience, and other criteria. Overall, we got through it holding our own in some of the easier categories and had a lot of fun. All the hard work and learning we had been through was truly starting to show.

Due to several things being out of our control, Deirdre and I were unable to plan a trip to meet my sister that year. Not to miss out riding together, my sister was able to haul her horse up and stay with us for three weeks and enjoy some of our trails. Over the three weeks she was here we managed sixteen rides covering about one-hundred and thirty miles of trails. We rode a different trail each day and still did not ride all the trails available. We also spent five days in the arena and worked on filling in some holes.

I planned the rides so that our first several trips would help condition her horse to our terrain. She came from a relatively flat region to the mountains of northwestern PA, and I wanted to make sure her horse was ready for some of the big hauls up and down before we jumped right into the fun.

I cannot lie about being proud to show my sister the trails we ride. There are trail systems all across this country of ours and every one of them is beautiful in its own way. When you ride all the time you sometimes start to take your own trails for granted. It is such a good feeling when you ride them with someone who has never been on them before and see their reaction.

The "F" Trail

————

A MONTH AFTER MY SISTER LEFT, Deirdre and I packed up the LQ and headed out by ourselves back to East Fork TN. It was our first long haul out alone. We spent eight wonderful days riding and exploring. There are always stories from every adventure, no matter how routine the adventure may seem. Sometimes you are lucky enough to have a story that is worth the time to share. This trip had one of those for sure.

The majority of the one-hundred and twenty-five plus miles of trails around the campground are on top of a plateau. There are at least a dozen stunning vista destinations you can ride to that overlook deep valleys and ravines. There are plenty of woods and trails to explore that take you past several old cabins and ponds, offering some really beautiful riding. But there is also a trail that takes you down into the ravine and back up the other side. The "F" runs basically north and south, and the trail is clearly identified as a more difficult ride by the campground.

On the third evening as we sat around discussing the next day's riding plan, we decided to take a look at the "F" trail more closely. The loop was just over thirteen miles long and eleven of those miles would be on the upper plateau. The 'F" trail itself was only about two and a half miles long. I brought up the topo of the area and compared it to their map. We determined if we started on "F" at the south end, we would descend eight-hundred feet to the bottom over a distance of about a mile. It looked like the majority of both descent and ascent would be about a 20% grade on and off. Based on the width and maintenance of all the other trails in this system, we decided it was worth checking out.

Arriving at the trailhead for "F" the next day we began our descent into the ravine. Though the trail was maintained for visibility it was not as tame as most of the trails up top. It required a slow, careful ride making sure the horses tucked often. But it was nowhere near the same category as the Hugo Meadows or the Falls, so we just slowly made our way down.

We ran into a maintenance crew about two-thirds of the way down as they finished clearing a tree fall. We stopped and chatted for a while and learned they were out to check and clear "F" that morning. Well, that was good news for us, so we held up for a bit and let them get a good distance ahead of us before we proceeded.

We made it to the bottom where we picked up Fern Camp Creek. The trail became intermittently visible as it followed the creek beds. It was obvious that during heavy rains this trail would be un-ridable. We tracked northwest until we reached Buffalo Cove. We then circled around the base of the spur to the northeast and followed that ravine to start our ascent out. Soon after we started to the northeast we ran into the maintenance crew again, this time trying to turn their side by side around. During our conversation, we learned the vehicle could not go any further on the trail, and they would have to approach it from the other end. They assured us the horses could get through just fine.

Moving further up the ravine along the creek bed we came across a humongous tree fall that covered the entire base of the ravine. Well now. Having encountered more than one major obstacle before in our short riding career, we knew that you never just turned back until you thoroughly analyzed the situation.

The tree had fallen right to left. There was no way we could get around it to the left. The top of the tree was too full, and the side of the ravine was definitely too steep to even consider it. We could not step over the tree, it was too big, so that eliminated any chance of going through the middle. That left the right side, and that did not look very pretty, either.

On the right side of the ravine, the mountain had a slope of about 30 degrees. To clear the base of the tree we would have to climb up about one-hundred feet then go back down. As for the terrain, it was littered with normal rocks, scrub, leaves and branches. Nothing we hadn't bushwhacked through before except it was on the side of a ravine.

Not being of the mind to turn around and head back, we closely analyzed the right side of that ravine for at least ten minutes, discussing and calculating possibilities. It would be tough, but if we started a little further back, it would give us a little clearer path and a less direct approach. We could ride up the side of the ravine at a shallower angle to a point twenty feet above the obstacle and immediately turn the horses back down, hopefully at another shallow angle to the trail on the far side.

Well, will you look at us. Thinking we are all smart and stuff down here in that ravine facing down a tree blocking our way. With a little more discussion on the particulars, Bobbi and I were on our way.

These are the moments that I have a hard time distinguishing between trusting my horse and just being plain ignorant. I typically lean heavily toward trusting my horse.

I lined her up to start up the side of ravine. Reins in my left hand up and forward, loose but not too loose. Lean forward and grab some mane. Push my seat to get going then get my legs off her body. BREATHE.

With a slight lurch, we started up the side of the ravine. On her second lunge up, I tell myself to sit that seat, move that core and ride that horse as she pushes and climbs up. My focus is ahead of her, on my turning

ROD WELLING

point at the apex of our climb, but at the same time I'm keeping a close eye on the immediate ground around us. BREATHE.

Several seconds later we reached the top and it was time to turn. I immediately noticed the descent was not going to be shallow at all, but more direct. A slight neck rein to the left, easy. Just barely touch the right shoulder with your leg and keep that left leg open. She started to give the shoulder. Now light left leg cue to the hip, EASY, and release. We instantly made the ninety degree turn and started down the other side. BREATHE.

Quickly Rod, keep that left hand as far forward as you can and let out a little more rein. Lean back as far as you can and keep those legs off her. Focus on guiding her only if you need to, but with soft, easy moves. Look where you want her to go and just let her do her thing. BREATHE.

We quickly arrived on the other side, and we were both alive. I loved on Bobbi like she had just won the Derby. I moved up trail and turned to watch as Deirdre came over the apex and began her descent. I was awestruck as I admired the equitation and performance as she and Jesse made it look like an everyday walk in the park.

Then we were both safely standing there on that trail in dead silence. We both just stared at each other, expressionless as our hearts raced in our chests and our minds sped through the last two minutes.

"Holy Shit." Deirdre finally broke the silence.

Well, aren't we just the riders of the year now. Bahaaaa!

I would like to say that was the last event on the "F" trail, but it wasn't. We were about halfway up the other side when we had to navigate another tree fall. This one was not even remotely as hard, but it did have a different twist to throw at us.

142

The trail had just leveled off some as it ran along the side of the ravine when we ran into the other tree fall. It was an easy up and around to the left and then back down on the trail except, unknown to us, the tree fell exactly where the trail turned ninety degrees to the right so when we came around there was no trail to go back to. Okay then.

Riding down where I thought the trail should be, I could see we were on a small rock outcrop about five feet high. That was why the trail turned right. Looking around I could see that the top edge of the outcrop continued away from us for about twenty feet then turned left, then looked like it just disappeared after about a hundred feet. I knew the trail was not going to go all the way back down into the ravine again, so I figured it might just circumvent the outcrop.

I was right. Where it looked like the top edge of the rock outcrop disappeared to the left, we found the trail and happily finished the thirteen-mile loop on the "F" trail without any more excitement.

We made our last trail ride on December 21ST that year, racking up about eight-hundred miles.

That's a Go for Throttles Up

E NTERING YEAR NUMBER NINE, we found ourselves in a pretty cool place compared to eight years earlier. We had made many new friends that we shared the trails with regularly. We have shared arena time with some really good riders who have taught us how to improve and with others who we have helped as well. Whenever I had the opportunity to watch our trainer working a horse, she would always take the time to explain what she was doing, why she was doing it and the results she expected. I started asking questions about technique and proper placement of cues. And for the first time in eight years, I could actually see what I was being told to look for.

Not to brag, but I think we may have reached the point where we 'almost' look like we know what we are doing. Nah, not really.

I would only ride one "Cowboy Only" clinic and one two-day clinic this year due to scheduling, but Bobbi and I were there. We were excited to ride with our favorite clinician and our trainer again. I was hoping to have finally gotten enough of my stuff together to ride a controlled canter for some of the exercises. It was time for Bobbi and me to strut our stuff.

The two-day Beginner Horsemanship clinic started, and the first day focused on working some good patterns at the trot. But the second day would be one for the records.

The second day of the clinic started out normally, with the first half hour spent on ground exercises then riding around to get the "fresh" off the horses. Bobbi was all cool and laid back with no signs of being fresh. Then we started the exercises.

I do not remember what our first exercise was, but the clinician had told us at our morning briefing he was going to ask the riders to step up their game and push a little outside of their comfort zone. I do like his style because he encourages you to try but doesn't set you up to fail. Anyway, I was excited I was finally going to canter by my choice in a clinic.

Bobbi and I sat calmly waiting for our chance as the riders each took their turns ahead of us. Then we were up. I remember we started out in a nice, steady trot for a bit, then he asked me to transition into a slow canter. This is what I had been working on all winter and I was ready; I was so ready.

So was Bobbi.

I set her up, brought my leg back, asked and we were off to the flipping races. Shades of the nine-cone pattern. Only this time I was not pulling and squeezing. All 16 hands of her and those long legs were running wide open. We were at the end of the arena in the blink of an eye and as we made that turn, all my weight was in the outside stirrup, so I didn't launch off her into the wall. I was riding her with my core just fine. I tried to slow my seat and give the whoa command, but I could not slow her down. I brought her into tighter and tighter circles until I finally got her down to a trot then a walk.

What heck was that? We had been doing this pretty well on our own. Okay, well let's try that again, maybe I miscued or something. I set her up to start the exercise again and we were off to the races again.

"Sit back. Get your hands down. Get your legs off her." I can hear the clinician hollering through the PA. Ironically, I was coherent enough to hear him and I thought I was doing it. Legs off no pressure, check. Lean back and ride with your core, check. Hands forward get some slack in the reins, check. Outside rein down and off the neck for speed, tap, tap, tap, check. Slow your seat to slow her down, check.

Again, I had to tighten the circle until she started too finally slow down. Well, that surely was not what I was hoping for that morning.

As we slowed to a walk, she was all about getting back over to the group. Knowing she can get a little 'herd bound' during clinics, I thought maybe not so much young lady, so took her off to one side away from everyone. Bobbi was all calm and good, standing there like nothing ever happened. Me? I chalked it up to a little burst of energy she needed to get out of her system. There were more exercises coming. She'd be fine.

Then again, maybe not. That went on all day long. She walked fine, would only work at a fast-posting trot, and when I asked for the canter, she was absolutely all in every time. By lunch, I think we had become the entertainment for the day. I learned later it was more like, "I can't believe he is still riding her through that" followed with chuckles and laughs by my fellow riders.

During the lunch break, I took the opportunity to ask my trainer for some insight. She had worked with Bobbi and me while practicing this, so she knew we could do it. She had watched that fiasco all morning, so I was hoping she would be able to enlighten me on what I was doing wrong. She told me she could not give me an answer about my riding, but she did tell me: "Some days, who knows what flies up their skirt?" Whew, now what? LOL

I am sure by the end of that day, the group had heard the clinician hollering, "Sit back. Get your hands down. Get your legs off" so many times it was permanently imbedded in their brains. But I did not give up. I absolutely refused to give up. And I refused to get frustrated with her. I knew this horse and I could do this. I had to be doing something to cause this.

The day was winding down, and once again Bobbi and I did our "Man o' War" (11) race around the arena not even remotely running the exercise pattern, so the clinician asked if he could ride her.

I gladly dismounted and relinquished her reins. Maybe he could tell me what was going on. I watched him mount up and do some turns and bends and softening exercises as he explained to all of us how important this was to control the horse. He told us to watch how much more relaxed she was, how willing she was to respond to his cues because she was softer. Watching them from the ground while holding his horse, I had to agree, she was nice and relaxed as he maneuvered her about. She was still relaxed as he got her into a trot.

He explained as he rode how nice and soft he was getting her, and how that was setting her up to comfortably and smoothly transition into a canter. He was telling everyone over the PA to notice how her demeanor had become softer and that now he was going to ask for the transition.

All the time I had spent watching and learning was about to pay me back in spades. I was able to see what other riders were doing and observe more than one thing as watched. I could see the hands, legs, and seat of another rider as they rode. And as the clinician and Bobbi rocketed around that arena, I did indeed watch intently.

A part of me so wanted to be a smart ass and yell, "Sit back. Get your hands down. Get your legs off her." As much as I know he would have found humor in that, I refrained.

I watched and waited until he got her into tighter and tighter circles to slow her down. I was eager to hear his professional evaluation of the ride and of my horse. Which basically amounted to, "She's a handful."

I faulted no one for that day. Not me, not the clinician, not my trainer and certainly not the horse.

At one point during that afternoon, as I sat on my horse waiting my turn and trying to figure out what was going on, a thought occurred to me. I ride a horse that absolutely loves to ride trails. She excels at it, and I trust my life to her. She and I spend ten thousand percent more time in the woods than we do in the arena. So where is she most comfortable? I would have to say on the trails. So, with that being said, if you were to take a multimillion dollar reining horse that has spent its entire life in an arena and put them on a trail for a day what would happen? I may be wrong, and I probably am, but I have a feeling it would be a little different horse than you were used to in the arena.

Now that was not an excuse, because I know Bobbi can work comfortably in the arena, but it kind of made me feel better.

That was a long, hard day in the saddle. She never did settle down, but we stayed the course none the less.

At the end of the day, I was relaxing with some of my fellow riders around the picnic table talking about the clinic. Someone complimented me on my determination that day. I guess I never really thought about it because I was focused on trying to figure out what I was doing wrong. The conversation turned into everyone sharing moments of Bobbi and me that were not funny at the time but are now great stories to share and laugh about. Then my trainer spoke up and told me she was impressed with the way I went back out every time with a fresh, clear head, focused on trying to figure out what was happening and not getting frustrated. I was humbled. That comment from her meant more to me than she will ever know.

So here is the best part of this memory. The very next day was the "Cowboy Only" clinic. And when I asked Bobbi to canter, if you had not seen her the day before, you would never have known she had any speed all. She was cool, collected, polite and perfect. Guess I better watch more closely what is flying around her skirt.

We would go on to have two long hauls out that year. One to Shawnee National Forest in Illinois and one to Big South Fork TN.

Just Something about a Horse

RIDING THROUGH A SECTION of the Lusk Wilderness in Shawnee National Forest that year was probably one of the most technical rides we had encountered so far. We found ourselves navigating big steps for the first time as well as very tight turns on very narrow trails while handling lots of other obstacles and challenges just to keep us humble. I think I used just about every finite maneuvering cue I knew during that hour and a half.

As we maneuvered through those challenges, I could not help thinking about how different my thought process was since riding in the Smoky's five years earlier. As I approached each obstacle in the Lusk Wilderness, I evaluated and determined my course of action. Sometimes I would discuss it with the girls, sometimes I would just ride it. I would ask my horse for a step, to move the shoulder, a quick jump up or bend around a tight point. All those little cues and requests allowed me to safely maneuver my horse and myself through the very difficult obstacles and terrain.

More than anything, I found myself focusing on only asking my horse for what I wanted at that moment and nothing more. If I wanted a slight hip, I asked for a slight hip making sure I was not putting pressure anywhere else that could send any other cue to her.

I found myself trusting. Trusting that she knew what I wanted. Trusting that she would perform her task. Letting her know that I trusted her.

I would wrap up the year riding about nine-hundred trail miles before we called it a season on the trails.

AS WE BEGAN OUR TENTH year the arena awaited us. Our new goals were already in place, we knew the holes we needed to fill and had a plan of action. We plan to continue to seek professional training and advice, attend more clinics, and head out to more seminars and shows. We booked two adventures for the upcoming year, one to the Ozarks in the spring and the other back to Big South Fork in the fall. I set a personal trail challenge for myself to try and ride one-thousand trail miles this year and I have committed to putting in at least one-hundred hours of arena time over the winter.

I have had some excellent help on my journey into horsemanship so far. Although my horsemanship has improved, I still have a long, long way to go. I suspect I always will.

I am also honest with myself and realize that in the grand scheme of things, I haven't come very darn far at all.

I have learned so much on this journey only to learn that I know so little.

Most importantly I have learned to first ask; "What am I doing?" before I look to the horse.

I have found that learning requires a strong commitment. A commitment to understanding the horse. A commitment to understanding myself. A commitment to accepting failure as a path to success. A commitment to putting in the time it takes. A commitment to spending time in the saddle refining my abilities.

I also now understand that I will never stop learning.

I constantly tell myself: *"We learn the most from our failures and retain best that which was the hardest to achieve. There is no loss in learning only the gaining of knowledge."*

I have no desire to compete competitively. I have no aspirations of being a trainer or a clinician. I don't suspect anyone will ever look at me and say, "Boy, I wish I could ride like him."

My deepest desire is to be able to continue riding trails as long and as safety as I possibly can. The only way I can be safer is to learn to be better.

At seventy-one I realized I cannot afford to put it off until tomorrow. I need to work on it today so that I will be able to ride tomorrow. Some days it seems like a dauntless task, but my motivation to continue riding drives me forward.

So, ride on cowboys and cowgirls and immerse yourselves in the joy of feeling your horse under your seat.

May you all experience at least once in your life that feeling you get when your horse gives you exactly what you need when you need it the most.

Above all else, believe.

"From my saddle life is a great adventure."

Acknowledgements

———

There are so many people who have helped me over the years to create all the countless memories and adventures it would be impossible to recognize them all. Anyone who has helped me, criticized me, corrected me, cheered me, laughed at me, ridden with me, or spent any time around horses with me, I thank you.

There are a few people however, I do need to mention, for without them I would have probably given up the first time I went to mount Montana and my butt never touched the saddle. Diane Burkey, DeeAnn Marsh, Traci Wade, Stuart Rybak and Linnea Campbell. You have all been such important pieces in my horsemanship puzzle over the years. Thank you all for everything.

Most importantly I want to acknowledge my wife, Deirdre. Without her none of this would be. You may task me woman, but you never let me sit around and rust. Thank you for having a dream and allowing me to be a part of it. Thank you for never letting me make the excuses that could come so easily. Thank you for pushing the buttons that make me dig in and do it. Thank you for all your support and help with this memoir. But most of all thank you for being my partner in life. You are my world, and you will be forever plus two.

Credits/Citations/Footnotes

Cover & Author Photo by: Deirdre Welling

Summer 2022

Cover-Bobbi and me. Author- Cisco, Montana and me

Rear Inside Cover Photo by: Stephanie Hoden-Nearing

Winter 2023

Cisco, Deirdre & Jesse, Bobbi & me.

0 - PF-FLYERS IS A Registered Trademark, New Balanced Athletics Inc.

1 - Holiday Inn Express is a trademark and brand of Six Continents Hotels, Inc.

2 - https://extension.psu.edu/horse-stable-manure-management

3 - From the song, Like a cowboy by Randy Houser

4 - https://www.fs.usda.gov/recarea/nfsnc/recarea/?recid=48922

5 - Duluth Fire Hose is a registered trademark of Duluth Trading Company®

6 - https://www.virginia.org/listing/virginia-highlands-horse-trail/6314/

7 - Aint No Mountain High Enough© Sony/ATV Music Publishing, Songwriters Nickolas Ashford/Valerie Simpson performed by Diana Ross

8 - Horse People Magizine

9 - Sir Winston Churchill

10 - EXCA ©Extreme Cowboy Association All Rights Reserved 2017

11 - Wikipedia: Man o' War was an American thoroughbred racehorse.

Copyright

About the Author

Mr. Welling is a retired septuagenarian enjoying his life trail riding and making memories with his wife and friends in northwestern Pennsylvania. The sound of a tinkling collar bell can be heard just about everywhere he goes announcing the presence of Cisco, his faithful Golden Retriever and "Trail Dog Extraordinaire," who is way more popular than the author.

www.ingramcontent.com/pod-product-compliance
Lightning Source LLC
Chambersburg PA
CBHW032133040426
42449CB00005B/215